FOR YOUR CONSIDERATION
THE COLLECTED ESSAYS OF JONATHAN CUE

JONATHAN CUE

Title Font 'Beau Rivage' designed by Rob Leuschke.

Author Font 'Garamond' designed by Claude Garamond.

Cover Art by Nanako Alexia Cook.

Graphic Design by Elizabeth Grey.

Formatting by Jody E. Freeman.

Compiled by Jonathan Cue. Obviously.

Everything else by Me. The one and only.

To the Old Gods above,
who's glory and wisdom lights the very stars themselves, and who's
providence was the guiding hand to so many of my own lessons.

This text and all lessons herein
were written in part meditation, part prayer,
for to find higher truths and insight is nothing less than a holy task, and we
become more divine in its pursuit.

Let us climb higher,
so that one day
our wisdom may light the stars too.

CONTENTS

IN DEFENSE OF FREEDOM OF SPEECH

his essay is inspired in part by the curtailing and repression of certain political groups across the world.

Such groups include: "Russians" (an Ethno-Political association based in Russian Nationalism and Anti-Immigration), outlawed by the Moscow court in 2015 ; the "Everything for The Country" Party, a far right political party banned in Romania in 2015; the 'Popular Force Party', a Mexican-Nationalist far-right party banned in 1948 ; "Kach", a far right Israeli-Nationalist party banned in 1994; the "National Bolshevik Party", a Russian based political party banned in 2007; "Vlaams Blok", a far-right Belgian party advocating for Flemish Nationalism, dissolved in 2004 ; and the "New Triumph Party", a far-right Argentine based political party banned in 2009.

Needless to say, I do not believe this curtailing is right. I may not agree with the ideologies espoused, but I also believe that freedom of speech and expression is a fundamental right in any free and just society. Indeed, the freedom to express yourself, your opinions, and your views with gusto is <u>necessary</u> for a free state, no matter how extreme, hateful, or radical those views may be.

If you disagree from the get-go, and think that these bans are justified due to the far-right and nationalist nature of the aforementioned groups, then I would ask you to rethink your stance since other such outlawed parties include left-leaning groups such as: The "PSPU" (or: "Progressive Socialist Party of Ukraine"), banned at the onset of the Russian invasion of Ukraine in 2022; the "Action for Change" party, a Mauritanian political party campaigning on the rights of Haratin peoples before being forcefully dissolved in 2002; the "Tudeh Party of Iran" (which was originally formed with the intention to integrate formerly British-colonial companies so that they were beholden to Iranian society and laws before being outlawed following a coup and liquidated with the arrest and execution of many of its key members in 1949), and "The Communist Party of Hawaii" (formed with the need of organized labour unions and non-violent strikes, and eventually declined in influence after seven of its head members were kidnapped by the FBI and charged with 'conspiracy to overthrow the territorial government' in 1951).

As it turns out, the laws and regulations used to suppress your foes are also the same laws that can be used to suppress *you* when your support is deemed no longer necessary.

Let me declare, first and foremost, that this only goes so far as banning groups on *ideological* grounds. I do not support violent methods of uprooting peaceful policy. I do not encourage hooliganism. And I do not support the plotting of criminal activity. Even the history of some of these groups I made example of are spotty; where they each, in their part, cry for their own innocence while the government who banned them insists it was justified; and it is difficult ferreting out the truth in each case.

Despite this, the point remains: If your group is banned because one of your friends punched a kid and you decided to harbour them, then tough for you; but I do not believe in guilt by association. When people suppress what they view as harmful rhetoric in favour of their beliefs and in-group, that is where I draw the line; because they often fail to understand that these laws *do not go away* once power has changed hands. They are *still* utilized, just to someone else's ends.

Just because a government is not currently tyrannical does not guarantee the next one will not be, and once given power, they are loath to give it up.

It is rather easy to always imagine yourself as being within the 'in-group', which I'm sure is exactly how Alan Turing of the British GCHQ felt in cracking the Axis' Enigma Machine and helping the Allies win WW2 before he was accused of homosexuality and indecency, ousted from his position, stripped of his honours, and forced to undergo hormonal therapy and chemical castration.

It is difficult to imagine that one might have their closest allies, those they helped win wars, turn their backs on them; but as the wise CGP-Grey once noted: The people you need to gain power are not the same ones you need to keep it. And I tell you, dear reader, that they need your support to instate these laws, not to maintain them. And that they will maintain them at *their* behest, not yours.

Before going forward, let us first make a certain distinction. A common argument against Freedom of Speech is that speech could be used to lie to the extreme detriment of others (such as with Libel: knowingly spreading falsehood in order to damage someone's reputation) or spread overt chaos (such as screaming "Fire!" in a crowded theater to cause a stampede). To this... I agree! I do not think these things should be allowed, as it would cause far greater harm to social cohesion as a whole than allowing them could help, just as I do not believe that groups who otherwise act as an organizer to extreme violence ought to be protected by free-speech laws.

But it's also disingenuous to pretend that that's what we're talking about here. When most people discuss 'Free Speech', what they're really discussing is 'Freedom of Expression', the ability to express your beliefs and opinions openly and without fear of legal repercussions; and that distinction is important. It should not be legal to claim a man beat his children in order to ruin his reputation. It SHOULD be legal to claim it is in *your opinion* that he *seems* like one who would beat his children; just as it should be legal to be *mistaken* in believing there was a fire in a crowded theater and unintentionally causing a stampede; because these are genuine beliefs and views rather than deliberate acts of malice and chaos (and just to incite more of that chaos, I will be using 'Freedom of Speech' and 'Freedom of Expression' interchangeably from here on out).

Sure, make it as illegal as you please to sow wanton chaos and discord, but the right to maintain and express beliefs that could *lead* to such chaos and discord absolutely must be protected.

Notably, many against the idea of free speech seem to be under the impression that their opponents are arguing FOR hate speech when this isn't often the case. I've met few who argue that you ought to encourage people to murder a man and have it be protected, nor have I met any who argue that you ought to be able to harass people until they reach a breaking point. Rather, we are arguing that the worst of us should be _allowed_ to speak so that the best of us are never silenced at the behest of another.

So, alright, now that that's out of the way, what is the middle-ground, then? For surely there must be a way to secure free speech while curbing extremism or hate speech, isn't there?

Well…

Not really, no.

The crux of the problem in trying to allow 'free speech' while curtailing hateful speech is that it depends entirely upon the view of the lawmaker as to what hate-speech actually is. There are varying definitions as to what counts as hateful or divisive speech, and that's excluding its raw dependence on societal norms to act as a buffer for what may be 'hateful' or 'divisive' in the first place. In modern times, it can be seen as hate speech to levy vitriol and slurs at African Americans, this is so, but during eras gone-by it was equally divisive to speak out in favour of the civil rights and liberties of the African American community; as Martin Luther King Jr. himself was once accused of extremism.

Or 'Pussy Riot', the pro-feminist, anti-authoritarian band in Russia who is regularly arrested for its divisive demonstrations and speech regarding the abuses of women and LGBT, and the administration's complete cover-up of it.

Or think of the status of Jews in Nazi Germany and how the government might have felt about you speaking out against the Holocaust. They would have been quite eager to use laws against such 'divisive' speech to make sure dissidents like you were silenced.

There are even unfortunate incidences where someone's speech had them removed entirely, not by the whims of the government, but from their own forum of expertise; and not for any misstatements or falsities within their research, but only due to their personal opinions completely outside of it; such as the case with Richard Dawkins where his invitation to speak at the 2016 Northeast Conference on Science and Skepticism was withdrawn because of his *"approving re-tweet of a highly offensive video"*, the video in question being a satirical comparison between Muslims and Feminists wherein he expressed his belief that the minority of both groups had much in common regarding their views on freedom of speech. An opinion which had nothing to do with the conference itself.

Before eventually retracting their decision, they initially went on record defending it, stating, quote: *"We believe strongly in freedom of speech and freedom to express unpopular, and even offensive, views. However, unnecessarily divisive, counterproductive, and even hateful speech runs contrary to our mission and the environment we wish to foster at NECSS."*

Personally I would have liked to see their example of unpopular, offensive speech that *couldn't* be considered unnecessarily divisive, counterproductive, or hateful. But they didn't include one, so I guess we'll never know.

In a free and just society, the *ability* to speak hatefully is, by definition, the measure of which you can speak freely. Your ability to say things that people do not like is directly correlated with your level of freedom of speech, whether it be against your peers, special interest groups, the upper classes, or your government. You cannot separate free speech from hate speech, and by trying to do so, you only undermine your own freedoms.

Before you consider banning the expression of hate-speech, you must understand that in order to remain unhypocritical, this would include all speech that could be considered hateful or inciting, even against those YOU consider hateful and inciting. There can be no picking and choosing here without getting wrapped up in tyrannical red tape over why it is okay to be hateful toward one group and not another. What a strange twist it would be to see Neo-Nazi's hauled off for hate speech only for you to be hauled off with them for saying they ought to be silenced.

"Goebbels was in favour of free speech for views he liked. So was Stalin. If you're really in favour of free speech, then you're in favour of freedom of speech for precisely the views you despise. Otherwise, you're not in favour of free speech."
- Noam Chomsky

Well, what of *vetted* speech, then? The idea that you may say whatever you like so long as it passes the checks and balances present to ensure it is non-hateful and reasonable! Unfortunately, even here we fall flat. To be in favour of vetted free speech is simply to be in favour of whatever speech the human, biased, sometimes incorrect experts approve of. To ask approved questions, cite approved sources, and arrive at the approved conclusions.

Then again, even experts can disagree with each other. So what then?

This all only goes so far as to include speech the government might actually deem hateful or divisive due to its own morality; and doesn't even touch on how such governments might abuse their powers to restrict critics of the state, political opponents, or those speaking out against them.

In Canada, for example, there is no such right guaranteeing Freedom of Speech as of this writing. In fact, the government reserves the right to jail you for speaking something that is objectively, absolutely true, based only on the grounds that it would be considered "*reasonable [and can be] justifiable [to limit your speech] in a free and democratic society*".

It was created in order to curtail the spilling of state-secrets during wartime and social disorder that comes through apocalyptic announcements, and yet if the government wished, speaking out against their crimes and the crimes of its politicians could easily count as something that would threaten a free and democratic society, couldn't it? In this way, you could scream "Fire!" in a crowded theater, trying to warn people of an *actual fire* that is *currently burning*, and **still** be suppressed because the reigning administration deemed it more harmful to alert the people and cause a panic than just letting the fire spread. The unfortunate implication being that your freedom of speech must be absolutely curbed *just in case* someone, somewhere, might say something against the status quo, unproductive or otherwise.

So too the same statement could be made toward any country that has suspiciously lengthy leadership and a marketed lack of media-published dissent. I wonder how many of them would consider it a far greater "threat" for people to be informed of their ill-doings than to actually protect people from the consequences of them.

. . .

In modern times, this kind of tactic of abusing the idea of peaceful decorum in order to limit criticism is used more frequently than one might expect. When Greta Thunberg spoke out to rally people against climate change, the whole of her detractors, some of whom actually levying legitimate criticism, were faced with a wall of backlash: *"She's just a child. Why are you attacking her?"*, as if 'disagreement' were synonymous with 'attack', and it dismissed any and all credibility your arguments had.

Or what of activist groups, who hide any wrongdoing, suspicious behaviour, or misuse of funds behind the defense that you are only pointing these things out because YOU are a racist, or a sexist, or a fascist, or a communist, or a "special snowflake".

For indeed, ALL sides use this tactic to dodge criticism and attempt to weasel out of my grasp, but as I so lovingly told my friend when they said I sounded like a Communist: "I could be fucking Karl Marx himself and it *still* wouldn't invalidate my criticism of the United States' predatory insurance scams."

Or to put it another way: Would you be right in beating a dog just because a Fascist said you shouldn't?

"The trouble with fighting for human freedom is that one spends most of one's time defending scoundrels. For it is against scoundrels that oppressive laws are first aimed, and oppression must be stopped at the beginning if it is to be stopped at all."
- H. L. Mencken

It sounds like it should all be so simple though. Most everyone agrees that being a douchebag isn't good, and we also agree that the listener, or watcher, or reader has rights to not be pied in the face by offensive material, so why can't it be a simple process to declare speech that is grossly offensive or deliberately provocative as in the wrong, remove it, and get on with our day?

The problem in letting the listener decide when speech should be curtailed is exactly as said; that it is the listener who decides who gets to speak, and about what; and we've all known someone in our lives who would rather we didn't speak at all, whether it be a pushy relative, an out-of-touch friend, or an invasive stranger.

What a member of an extremist theocracy considers hateful is going to be far different than what a militant activist considers hateful; and when they clash, or even when they don't, when they are simply up against the common man who does not share their views, who among them gets to declare which others have the right to speak? Even the obvious answer of the moderate man is not so obvious if you look back over ten years of culture, or twenty, or thirty, and see how much the norms have changed since then. The Overton Window. A moderate in your grandfather's time may well be considered an extremist now, and vice versa.

Just as well, even *supposing* someone were being deliberately provocative, would you not wish to call them out on it and rise to the defense of the ideals you held dear? Would it not be a disservice to all parties involved, then, if they needn't respond at all, but simply declare you as an agitator and have you removed from the forum?

Could the same not be said for this book? So rife with my opinions.

Am I not a provocateur?

If not, why not? What is the distinct difference? And more importantly, who gets to *decide* what this difference is? For I am forced to remind you, reader, that if you believe such things as: Women should have rights, or: People should not be enslaved, or even: People should be able to learn to read if they want to, then you are expressing what was, at one point, a hateful, offensive, dangerous, divisive, counter-productive, and overall galling belief; and the only reason you can be secure in speaking those beliefs now is because others have suffered for it before you. People from before your time stood up to *declare* these things, come what may. But if they were silenced by the very points that critics of free speech espouse, where would we be now? And what of one hundred years from now? What beliefs do you hold that will be considered barbaric then?

You see a major crux of my argument then; it's not that hate speech or extremist agitation shouldn't be limited, but rather that putting the power of jurisdiction in **anyone's** hands to decide who may or may not speak is a very dangerous game to play, and will do far more harm in the future than any slur or radical speech could do in the now.

Even things like war or pandemic exceptions to basic rights can be a slippery slope. It was not too long ago that Canada and America used World War 2 as a justification for interning a massive portion of people for no other reason than Japanese-ancestry; an act we can now all see to be an abuse of powers and a crime against one's own citizens.

It is very convenient to admit actions were wrong in retrospect, long after any call for accountability need be made. It is much more impactful to call for concern over actions while they're actually happening.

Plus, there is that old adage, isn't there? *"If you allow the government to curb your rights in an emergency, they will invent emergencies to curb your rights."*

"A law that can be directed against speech found offensive to some portion of the public can be turned against minority and dissenting views to the detriment of all."
  -Anthony Kennedy

There are some that will point out, rather accurately, that speech is already limited, so what's the harm with limiting it more? To which I return that exact part of their own sentence: That greater harm comes from limiting it more.

Laws exist -ideally- in order to create an orderly society with as little friction as possible; but much like with the war on drugs, or seeing the state of constant lobbying, or spending an hour interacting with a Homeowner's Association can tell you: too many regulations and laws can easily be the CAUSE of friction, rather than reducing it. We don't have laws and regulations for the sake of having them, but to create order with as little fuss as possible. If they disrupt social order too much, or protect the wrong people, or encourage disorder, then what's the point?

But I am not representing both sides well. There are legitimate arguments to be made against Freedom of Speech, far more legitimate than a simple "I think it's bad." There have been great thinkers who saw unbridled free speech as an issue. So very well. We shall examine these arguments here.

One such argument, made by Kate Harding writing for Dame Magazine, notes that unmoderated and unrepressed speech may be fine for more moderate topics, but the more controversial a topic (or those speaking on it) become, it naturally follows that the more impassioned and agitating the forum will be. Fair enough.

Her proof of this extends further; in that after posting a few articles criticizing sexist fueled e-violence, many detractors responded by posting torture-porn in the comments of the article.

Lovely.

Though the editors could manually ban those posting said comments, nothing could be done over the extensive use of burner accounts people used to keep coming back to post. And here the story gets worse, because no amount of letters or emails sent to corporate ever provided a tangible solution to this problem. It was only when the editors went to Twitter to complain openly about the harassment they were facing and the lack of action by their parent company that something was finally done.

. . .

Her solution is simple: Moderate speaking-houses so that only those who are allowed to speak *can* speak, for much like how a publishing house NOT publishing drivel isn't limiting free speech, not being allowed to comment on an article isn't inherently limiting yours. You can still speak about it all you wish... elsewhere. To this I say:

I totally agree. Absolutely. If someone were in your house shouting slurs, and so you kicked them out, you are not limiting their free speech. We already discussed that those viewers, listeners, and readers have rights as well, and this includes not being disrupted in the same way that it should not be legal to disrupt those enjoying a nice movie by convincing them that there is a fire afoot.

However, even in this there should be mindfulness. By all means, moderate your own forums the way you please; but there is a vast difference in deciding on what standards ought to be said in your own circle where people can voluntarily hop in and out of versus the standards *all of society* should follow; and remember that if you endorse this idea of moderation to the standard of the moderator, you would have to give up your advocacy on closing forums that allowed hate speech. For that is ALSO to the taste of the moderator.

Furthermore, as Harding regrettably found; arguing against the moderators OF these forums as to who should be allowed to speak often does not bode well, and you must go to outside soap boxes to have these problems addressed. So what if there are no outside soap boxes to go to? There is little secret as to how insular silicon valley is in its views.

If someone can decide on a whim that your views should go unheard; silence you on their platform, and then talk to their friends so that you cannot go on any other platform to speak elsewhere either, that does begin to seem as if it encroaches on one's ability to express themselves without recourse. Especially since many platforms do not offer just speech as a service, but many others coupled along with it. Games. Communities. Points to spend. Commerce. Markets. There are many who's businesses are exclusively online. All of this is a great stake of incentive to conform and can quickly spiral from simply muting someone to actively diminishing their livelihood; and I don't think someone should be denied a paycheck because they don't share the Correct Opinions™.

Natalie Regoli writing for 'ConnectUS' notes that Freedom of Speech can lead to abuses such as: The spreading of false information, the incitement of violence, the incitement to mob mentality, excessive verbal abuse, and the polarization of society at large, to which I say:

Yes. Yes it does. These are natural negative consequences to free speech in the same way that your car running out of gas is a negative consequence of driving it. Even things unilaterally beneficial to society often come with their own share of problems. There is no policy wholly good or wholly bad, neither objectively nor certainly by the court of opinion. The solution isn't to do away with these boons all-together, but to work on solutions that mitigate the problems.

Because we currently sow seeds under the watchful eyes of an imperfect administrative body, the forced correction of these aspects may just do more harm than good. There are a thousand pages worth of environmental and commercial reforms where, in the government's attempts to fix damage, they simply cause more.

Besides, living in a world where you can be jailed for attending anti-war protests or for criticizing those who push for military intervention over claims of Weapons of Mass Destruction sounds much bleaker than a world where people can just lie to you for fun.

There is also the argument that hate speech must be curbed so that violence cannot be expressed or condoned, and I'm going to go against many of my contemporaries and actually agree that speech *can* lead to violence. An idea that cannot be expressed to the masses cannot be followed by them. In any Orwellian world, this principle still stands: You cannot be free if you cannot express the ideas that lead to freedom. So it follows that you cannot be violent if you cannot express the ideas that lead to violence.

But there is a stark difference between an idea that can *lead* to violence and one that *encourages* it. José Rizal, a pioneering figure for democracy, pacifism, and education in the Spanish controlled Philippines was a figurehead of the revolution that led to his countrymen fighting for independence, and yet he himself never advocated for violence against these colonizers. He encouraged gentle resistance, of independence gained not through blood, but through a preferential relationship where Spain and the Philippines could be economic partners rather than oppressor and oppressed; and yet because many of his peers chose to act in violence anyways, they took Rizal's message as one of violence outright and condemned him to death through a firing squad. Socrates himself shared a similar fate, being made to drink hemlock after a high council condemned him on principle of what his ideas *could* lead to.

People cannot dominate one another. You cannot sap a man of his free will and have him act and think according to your wishes. We can police ourselves and try to make our statements as clear and concise as can be, but much like with the interpretation of religious text to justify wanton violence, or objective scientific discoveries being used as fuel for bigoted parties, so too can ANY statement be misinterpreted, either willfully or ignorantly, by supporters or opposition, to be condoning of violence.

I have heard too that Free Speech must be regulated because one's ability to speak and judge is a skillset rather than an inherent right; and that much like you would want only skilled craftsman to take on the role of building a road, so too would you only want those trained in philosophy and rhetoric to speak openly.

On the surface, this makes a great deal of sense. You *wouldn't* want an untrained craftsman building a road. But I retort that roads are a necessity to an ever-growing society and economy. Even if there are no trained craftsman available, you *still* need the roads. To this end, even if there are no trained craftsmen, you would *still* have them built with whoever you could muster, and hope for the best.

So too, in this vein, is free speech necessary to an ever-growing society with ever evolving ideals and principles; and since we cannot wait for each individual to be trained in rhetoric, we must allow all to speak openly as their sensibilities dictate, for stagnation and ruin are greater threats than conflicting ideas or mistruths.

Personally, I'd just have rhetoric be a highschool course.

The magic of open discourse is that, yes, it allows people to be inflammatory if they choose, but it also allows listeners to be self-selecting. Admittedly, this is not a perfect solution. Despite what some may claim, free speech doesn't necessarily lead to more honest and open discussion. Many people wiser than we have been charmed by sweet words and snake oil.

An argument need not necessarily be <u>correct</u> to be *convincing*.

But even so, this method has a distinct advantage. People don't have to listen to a racist podcast if they don't want to. They can leave a stadium where the host speaks in favour of slavery. You, here, can toss my book into the nearest harbor if you do not like what I have to say (though if you're reading the e-book version, I'd suggest not); and this is compounded by the rights we have to force others from our homes, or report bad behaviour to the reigning moderators. The scenarios where you may be **forced** to endure verbal abuse tend to be few and far between and are usually allowed to happen due to fault in the administrative process.

And this method of unregulated self-selection is far superior to anything mandated by the powers that be. If you happen to disagree with that, because the powers that be happen to be on 'your side' and you like that sort of thing, then I would encourage you to stretch your imagination and think on how it might be if the side you *didn't* like had the exact same intention; to field an office that would mandate fact from fiction and regurgitate only approved information into your mouth, little baby bird, and how horrifying it might be if, say, a particular political or media demagogue had full control over your flow of information and used it only to their benefit.

This is, rightfully, terrifying; and it is no less so just because it is 'your side' doing it, and no amount of *"But my side are the good guys and they wouldn't do that!"* excuses it.

"Whatever crushes individuality is despotism, by whatever name it may be called and whether it professes to be enforcing the will of God or the injunctions of men."
  - John Stuart Mill

On December 3rd, 2012, at the Cambridge Union, England, during a debate titled: "This House Believes that Hate Speech is Not A Human Right", the speaker, part of the 'Pro' (that is to say -limiting hate speech) team, made an anecdote about a man alluded to be Andrew Brons.

Mr. Brons, if you do not know, is largely credited as being a Fascist; due to the fact that he galivants about in far-right parties in the UK, has some controversial views regarding race and immigration, and has edited journals with people who themselves participated in controversial movements or wrote mean books. The cherry on top of it all is that Brons is perhaps rightfully called a Fascist because, despite at the time of writing being seventy-five, he joined a Neo-Nazi movement at the ripe age of seventy...een. Seventeen. Pardon me. I sneezed while typing that. It was a decision he went on to lament in every interview that asked him about it.

Mr. Brons was supposed to join the debate that night in favour of the 'Con' (that is to say -favouring free speech) team, but was promptly disinvited after the Cambridge Union received a letter from NUS calling that he be removed because, paraphrasing:

"Once fascism had abused the democratic system and used its ability to have

its voice heard to silence the voices of others, it soon closed down any freedom to present any resistance."

I like to think they saw the irony and had a little giggle over it, but I doubt it.

The speaker went on to proudly proclaim, quote:

"That (in reference to the prospective views of Mr. Brons) this is what this side of the house opposes, it opposes any perspective that would silence the voices of others."

And I know they didn't see the irony because there was no giggling about it to be had.

Someone on the floor seemed to take issue and spoke out, though I could not hear what was directly said, and the speaker responded:

"We do not propose silencing the voices of people. We propose silencing a single idea."

The fact that it took disallowing a person to speak in order to silence this alleged idea didn't seem to make a difference.

Now whatever your views on Mr. Brons or how foolish it seems to openly lament joining a Neo-Nazi movement only to go on to associate with OTHER former Neo-Nazis, sure, that's fair, but I'd like to make a point to the Cambridge Union that Mr. Brons wasn't disinvited over what he did say, but over what they thought he **might** say. Of the views he **might** expound. By guilt of his associations. By the ideas they believe he represented.

I do not agree with their decision. I think I'd rather have liked to hear what he had to say on the subject, considering his own authoritarian leanings and whether or not free speech is actually something he would support in his idealized society, why, and to what ends, but I can't because he was disinvited and I'm not allowed back in Britain for another two hundred and eighty-five years.

In all of this, in their rescinding his invitation and the reasoning besides, it provides the clearest example of what I've been talking about this whole time: That we cannot try to ban hate-speech in any federal, administrative, or organized way, because it is not and has *never* been about what you say, but always about what they think you MIGHT say; to judge on behalf of an untold future of what hateful speech you might spew.

The Cambridge Union disinvited Mr. Brons because they believed it was the right thing to do, I get it, these are not malicious actors, they are trying to do the right thing; but Mr. Brons believes he's right too. That's why he holds the beliefs he does. BECAUSE he believes them to be right. Even as we accept that it is impossible for all of our beliefs to be correct, we still hold on to each of them because we believe they are. But so too does the KKK, so too did the Nazis, so too did the bombers spraying Agent Orange in Vietnam. No group acts believing they are in the wrong. They ALL wear the shroud of nobility, and they will do anything they have to in order to ensure their noble idea takes root. No matter how awful. No matter how tyrannical. No matter how terrible, and it is *because* it is this easy that it is all the more important to let people speak.

Because we *might* be wrong. But we'll never know unless we're willing to hear *why*.

"*A person should have the right to speak. A person should never be told they cannot speak. We only say (that the) one thing they cannot say is that other voices should not be heard.*"

How sour it tastes to hear this from your mouth, Mr. Speaker, and not from the mouth of an absent Mr. Brons.

. . .

There were other points raised at this debate. *"We're not talking about dissent, we're talking specifically about hatred,"* which on the surface makes sense. These are two very different types of speech, and you can theoretically allow one while disallowing the other. My point is, and has always been, that it is startlingly easy to lump them together; and it is even easier to pretend to equate the two regardless when the guilty party wishes to deflect criticism. Or, in a more pointed example: There has been a rising number of cases of people facing legal trouble over not affirming a trans person's gender identity. Is this act one of dissent against a perceived system that encourages mental illness, abuse, and dysphoria? Or is their lack of affirmation one of bigotry toward individuals who are harming no one and just trying to live their own lives the way they see fit?

These things are difficult to parse, because criticizing a behaviour is to criticize those who engage in it. To criticize a system is to criticize those who enforce it. Even a playground insult: "That's stupid," can be interpreted as 'You are stupid and thus did that', or 'Doing that makes you stupid'.

Dissent, by its very nature, is hateful; for it stems from a place of dissatisfaction and discord against the status quo. Though dissent can be born out of magnanimous motivations, there is no magnanimous dissent.

"Without free speech no search for Truth is possible; without free speech no discovery of Truth is useful; without free speech progress is checked, and the nations no longer march forward towards the nobler life which the future holds for man. Better a thousandfold abuse of free speech than denial of free speech. The abuse dies in a day; the denial slays the life of the people and entombs the hope of the race."
– Charles Bradlaugh

So fine, hate speech cannot be curbed without the strict limitation of the freedom of opinion and expression, that must be accepted, but so be it. Some are willing to bite the bullet because preventing extremism and radical gatherings and schools of thought is worth it. Ultimately, hateful rhetoric allows for hateful action to take place, and it is worth it to take those long-term risks and allow that some freedoms may be limited so that all can be safe in the now, right?

Not quite.

It is a crime to propagate 'hateful symbols', 'hate speech', and holocaust denial in Germany (effectively making being a member of a Neo-Nazi organization illegal), and yet since 2012 onward, it seems 'far-right ideals' have slowly been on the rise, culminating with a grand increase in the year 2020; with "Far-Right" associated crimes up by nearly 6%, crimes associated with antisemitism up nearly 16%, and a staggering 73% increase in anti-immigrant associated crimes, all up from 2019 as reported by AP News, and this is all despite the increasing restrictions and crackdowns the German administration has put in place, including the banning of far right organizations such as 'Combat 18', and increasing raids against other groups such as 'Reichsbürger'.

There is a similar story with America's 'Communism Control Act' of 1954, banning the Communist party and criminalizing its membership and support, an act that is still in effect today, not that you'd notice, with a rough one third of all millennials in the U.S having an 'Approving' view of Communism, as noted in a 2018 YouGov poll, and 70% of millennials saying they were likely to vote for a Socialist political candidate, as reported by the Independent.

Anyone familiar with the Satanic Panic or the media blacklisting of early 'gangster' culture can tell you that when a film, book, song, or activity is banned, far from losing steam, it GAINS it as a form of counter-culture, gaining notoriety BECAUSE of the ban rather than despite it; and with the failure of prohibition movements and the 'war on drugs', we have historical precedent to see that it spurs an underground movement wherein these things can easily flourish and gain more power.

That is not to say, of course, that outlawing things cannot have the intended effect. I'd presume more people would get murdered if murder were legal, and there are historical cases of cults/ideologies/groups being dissolved because the law made it too difficult to gather and spread their ideas. Rather, it is only to say that it is an *unreliable* method; and can often make an ideology far stronger, such as the case with Christianity in Ancient Rome.

So, when attempting to effectively curb hate-speech, what can we do about it?

When Political Science Professor Brendan Nyhan of Dartmouth College undertook the task of seeing what arguments successfully convinced anti-vax parents to vaccinate their children, he and his team discovered a bleak truth: That there were no pro-vaccination messages curated by the Public Health Authorities that reliably convinced the parents to vaccinate.

And yet, we can see where people CAN be convinced. Everything from the analysis of Youtuber 'Counter Arguments' and from the professional techniques used in rhetoric reflects the core idea that people's minds are rarely changed through evidence or passion, but instead through connection. To be heard, and so being willing to hear others in turn. Studies into deradicalization programs headed by the American Psychological Association and the journal: *"The Psychology of Radicalization and Deradicalization"* by Arie W. Kruglanski and their team have found that a fundamental aspect of turning someone from an extremist into a moderate revolves around, not empirical evidence or arguments, but just a genuine human connection where they find fulfillment and purpose outside of the group.

There is no better living proof of this than Daryl Davis, an African American R&B and Blues musician who, through simply trying to talk to members of the KKK and treat them with civility, has earned the respect and robes of many, now *former,* members; all of whom cite Mr. Davis' friendship as the direct reason for their disillusionment with the group. In this, it was never the arguments stated or statistics supplied or studies cited, but that same human connection that Professor Kruglanski found so important in breaking the insulation of hate-groups. Which is also why I'm writing this! Because I care about you! I hope that comes across and helps to convince you.

It may be true that the allowance of an idea will allow that idea, hateful or otherwise, to proliferate; but it will ALSO inevitably result in more moderate views that contradict it. It is not as if you can convince someone they will be heard and understood if you threaten to arrest them over what they express to you. Professor Nyhan found the same thing, that one of the only things that seemed to convince others out of their dug-in beliefs about vaccines were those close to them getting it and showing that they were fine.

In all of this, the pattern is clear. The greatest factor in curbing extremism and hateful ideology was not in refusing to allow them to speak, but in allowing them to be spoken *to.*

Finally, in regard to hate speech itself, I earnestly believe that such speech has value. Any experience can teach you something. Mr. Davis cites his own childhood memory of having things thrown at him by white supremacists as a formative experience in questioning how people can hate him without knowing him; a question that he went on to do an incredible amount of good in trying to answer.

People lose friends or relationships, sometimes over silly mistakes and sometimes over a divergence in life goals, and yet we can grow from it. The loss of a pet can help us learn how to let go. The loss of a competition can teach humility. The things we take time to make can be destroyed and yet there is still value in making them. I can get high and shit myself and be banned from the only Walmart within walking distance, and this teaches me that I shouldn't do drugs.

Look, the point is: negative experiences are an inevitability of life; and are just as much of an intrinsic part of life as positive experiences are. Sadness, anger, fear, and regret have just as much a place in our lives as happiness, love, courage, and hope. These things are not simply aspects we must endure, but things life is made better for facing. Things that give life its conflict and contrast, and sometimes even its meaning.

To be called ugly by one person only to be called beautiful by another, to be screamed at by one person only to be treated gently by another, to go through a hard day and then go through a great one, for one friend to abandon you only for another to be there when you didn't expect them to, for one person to bully you only for another to appreciate and love all the ways in which you are pleasantly strange. When we learn from these experiences, they not only make us well-rounded people, but they also make us *better* people.

To bring this essay to its close, I will return to that debate at Cambridge, when the Speaker went on to quote Karl Popper's paradox of tolerance, paraphrasing:

"Unlimited tolerance must lead to the disappearance of tolerance. If we extend unlimited tolerance even to those who are intolerant [...] then the tolerant will be destroyed, and tolerance with them. [Not that we must suppress them] But we should claim the right to suppress the intolerant, if necessary, even by force; for they may forbid their followers to listen to rational argument, [by claim that] it is deceptive, and teach them to answer arguments by the use of their fists or pistols."

In this I am reminded once more of all the movements for Social Justice that somehow, inexplicably, resulted in harm done to innocent people, such as 'Punch a Nazi', 'BAMN!', and others.

It makes me rather grumpy to hear such quotations from this side of the debate, the same side that proposed the defining factor for 'Hate Speech' ought to include the power to act on it so that marginalized groups are protected rather than targeted over anti-speech laws, and then immediately proposed putting people in jail over their words right after. Because nothing screams that you have 'Power' like people being allowed to make imminent threat to your freedom and livelihood.

And this all just gets back to exactly what I was talking about before; how easy it is to decry hate-speech, to come up with your own definitions, to create your own legal basis for prosecuting it, when you are so utterly certain that you are in the right and everyone else must bend to you, and the fact that people living in different cultures or who came a generation before us have radically different social norms, going all the way back down the line, with each new generation subsequently believing their own shitty ideas are the proper basis of morality and ethics and their dumb old ancestors didn't know better, is conveniently lost on these people.

That by sheer dint of... what? Genius, insight, perhaps even force of will, these Übermensch crossed into the final frontier of social morality as to what is absolutely right and objectively correct, whose beliefs shall never be found to be archaic or harmful in any way whatsoever going forward; how lovely, whatever shall we do without them?

It is easy to think that this, now, whatever ideas we have are right, and has always been, even if we are just now realizing it.

It is much more difficult to understand that people have believed that, earnestly, with every fiber of their being, LONG before now. And will for long after.

East, West, A.D, B.C, Fascist, Anarchist, Capitalist, Communist, Axis, Allies, Old, Young; it doesn't matter. You're going to be hard-pressed to find the man who doesn't earnestly believe that ALL he believes is right. Why would they believe it otherwise?

To believe that hate-speech ought to be limited is to believe that one of these people, ANY of these people; ought to be able to decide what you do and do not have a right to express.

I do not want a white supremacist to have legal jurisdiction over what I can and cannot say, just as I do not want a black supremacist to decide it. I do not want some snotty punk with British cultural values to have legal jurisdiction over me, just as I do not want some Appalachian Mountain Man to have it. I do not want a Communist to tell me what literature I can read, just as I do not want a Crony-Capitalist to. I don't want a religious extremist to tell me what views I can listen to, just as I don't want a forum moderator to tell me so.

From top to bottom, tip to toe, the only one who should decide what you can or cannot say and hear is *you*.

If you're earnestly trying to protect people, don't enforce limitations. Enforce warnings for potentially offensive things, but STILL let people decide for themselves what they want to hear.

Otherwise the only views you're trying to protect are your own. That you are so right, so correct, so righteously absolute, that nobody should be exposed to any worldview but yours. And I don't want you to have the power to decide that either.

In conclusion: All reasonable people know what hate speech truly is, so let us dictate for ourselves what we agree and disagree with. Let us decide for ourselves what opinions we deem worth listening to and which we do not. This is for us, as individuals, to decide; not corporations with a vested interest to do it for you, not a government that's bias toward its own perpetuation, and not special interest groups with a motive to interpret the world on your behalf. Decide for YOURSELF what is hateful and to be discarded and what is meaningful and to be listened to. And though this may allow bigotry to manifest and though this may allow violence to erupt, know that bigotry and violence are inevitable. It will never be curbed by policy or pity, for the blackest hearts do not care and the revolutionary will burn at the chains. Know that this is for us to decide, us to keep watch on, and for us to fight when fighting comes, because if violence is inevitable, it is better to clash for the sake of ideals than policy.

Anything less will not promote speech. Anything less will not encourage the soft-voiced to stand tall or the hard-hearted to sit quiet. Anything less will not protect you. Anything less will not truly filter what is worth seeing or hearing. It will only allow others to cover your eyes and ears and decide it for you.

We all have to live on this rock. We should all have a say in the direction it's headed. And if you disagree with me... that's fine. How lucky we are, that we live in a time and place where we can debate our views and work together to come to the right conclusions, instead of only the approved ones.

ON THE COLLAPSE OF SOCIETIES

*O*nce, when I was a young lad, I saw a little newspaper comic strip. I do not know who made it, though I do remember it vividly. It depicted four men in a boat, with the boat sinking due to a leaky hole.

The hole is only on one side of the thing, and so is sinking at that end first. The two men on that end, dressed as blue-collar joes, are struggling to bail out the water while the other two men on the other side of the boat, dressed in professional (one might say 'Political') attire, jib and jibe about how lucky they are that the hole isn't on their end.

The joke, of course, is that they're all in the same boat, will sink all the same, with the two men on the farther side of the boat being completely oblivious to their imminent peril.

It is a nice little thing. Adequate on the corner of a column.

It is also a misnomer. Named incorrectly. Meaning missing the mark.

The comic fails as it ascribes the indifference of the two men at the far end as due to ignorance, or stupidity. That people (though it is more apt to place the description toward those who hold more sway over society and its direction at large, so that is who I will be referring to henceforth) do not act to bail out the water because they do not know; that they misunderstand, or mishear, or are misinformed as to the truth; that perhaps they would jump at the chance to assist if only they knew that their inaction was dooming the ship.

But they wouldn't. That's the problem.

Let us suppose this ship is bigger, much bigger, a veritable cruise liner, holding 1000 people proper. Enough to have a micro-society onboard to better match our own. Suppose in this hypothetical example, that people act and react just as they do in regular society at large; suppose they gamble, and drink, and dance, and fall in love all on the waves of this choppy sea.

The only difference being that each individual has what we call "Resources". These resources have one very specific purpose, and that is to repair the ship when it leaks. Resources can be traded for goods and services, the time you have in a day could be fashioned into resources; even your arms, legs, and mental fortitude can become resources if you find the right outlet. The word 'Resources' is just a sort of catch-all term for things you want. A 'currency', if you will.

(Note: I am not referring to the catch-all term as 'currency' wholesale because I do not want this to become an anti-capitalist essay. I am not only referring to money here. I am referring to much of anything one might ascribe value toward; be it time, physical labour, popularity, or yes, even currency).

On this boat, people are valued based on their resources. The more resources you have, the more valuable you are to the boat and those on it. They are more willing to pamper you, appeal to you, compliment you, service you, all under the hope that you will share some of your resources, and the expectation that when the boat begins to leak, you will give up some of your resources to help fix it.

Simple, right?

There's a catch though, a sentence you might have missed on your first go:

"On this boat, people are valued based on their resources."

This means that there is a direct, intrinsic cause and effect; that when the boat finally leaks, and you use some of your resources to plug it up, you will suddenly find people pampering you a little bit less. Appealing to you a little less. Complimenting you a little less. Caring about what you think a little less. Caring about the state of your quarters, your entertainment, and your nourishment, a little less.

This is done because you hold less sway. Obviously. You have fewer supplies, and so you matter that much less. The elderly matter less. The poor matter less. The unpopular matter less. The weak matter less. The physically disabled matter less. The mentally ill matter less. The marginalized matter less. Those who cannot vote matter less. And you matter that much less because you now have, or have always had, less resources to spend toward any further problems that arise; and when you are less necessary, *you are less necessary.*

In short, those with the more supplies are treated well, and those with the less are treated poorly. Bang-On. This is often why you can find seemingly counterintuitive protocols on this boat; things like governments giving bailouts to massive corporations while letting the lower and middle classes rot in debt.

This is because these mega-corporations have something to offer, while the lower classes do not. They do not matter. Their thoughts, feelings, and opinions do not matter, because they can neither use their resources to help the government and because they lack the resources to vent their dissatisfaction in any way that matters.

Why would you give the same amount of pampering and sweetness and notice to someone who can only fix the smallest holes as you would to someone who can fix the biggest?

Do not be too hard on them. It is not just an issue of costs and gains, for it is no different to how you would treat someone who was being a dick to you versus how you would treat them if they were being a dick to you whilst holding a gun to your head. Something about urgency and the ability to decide someone's fate or how their day goes tends to bring out the geniality in people; and they are always more willing, and decisive, in helping those who can directly supply their comforts, power, or security. For if you treat everyone equally, what incentive is there to be a friend over a foe?

This is why you can find events like The Great Stink of 1858, where, after decades of imploring from the working class who lived beside it, the Parliament of England finally did something about the rampant, noxious fumes flooding from the river-turned-sewer Thames only because it got to the point where the nobility could smell it.

This is why the Sengoku Jidai period of Japan was so rife with betrayals, backstabbing, and opportunism; so rapidly did the power of clans wax and wane.

This is why many governments will crack down and put extra restrictions on new, budding businesses to favour larger corporations, as it is most certainly not the small businesses who sponsor these politicians come election time.

This is why when The Brothers Gracchi ran for the Roman senate on populist principles, the elites and upper class were able to turn the very populous the brothers fought for against them, by installing candidates who simply promised more goodies to the people than the brothers could.

This is why pretty people often have the 'Halo-Effect'.

And so it goes, on and on, and when people have finally used up their usefulness, they are often discarded. The politician does not run on policies suited to children, not because they are bad ideas (though ice-cream for breakfast certainly would be) but because children cannot *vote* for them. It is the principle in the simplest form. You can provide nothing? Your needs are not considered. You have *already* provided your resources and a new problem has risen that you cannot solve? Then someone who *can* solve it will take your place.

In this, the true 'collapse' comes from the fact that even those who can see the leaks in the boat, and the cracks they cause, and have the knowledge that it is going to get worse lest they patch it up; often have very great incentives NOT to do so. On top of being pounced upon by their peers, their offices and powers could easily be snatched up by rivals, and they cannot depend upon a populace, so easily swayed, to push them back into a position of power after a sacrifice is made on basis of that sacrifice alone. And thusly, when sacrifices do come, it is always the most virtuous, just, and righteous who give, before they are then trampled under the muck by the more vicious, conniving, and greedy, who retained their power and status to the last, and can now use it to keep others in the muck to ensure their position is never threatened.

Because that's the thing. If you are ONLY valued based on your resources, and goals as simple as staying relevant, staying in charge, or even just staying alive are entirely contingent on you NOT giving up your resources... Then why would it matter when the boat begins to sink? The professional who does not train their apprentice, the rulers who elect on loyalty over skill, the abusers who disallow the victim from any modicum of independence; all of these are examples of people trying to *keep* their resources even as the ship continues to sink.

And it is easy to point and laugh and say these people are stupid for valuing their position over a floating ship, but these people *know* the ship is sinking. They just don't *care*. They do not care because they know if they sacrifice all of their resources to repair the holes, they will be relegated to the absolute lowest tiers of dankness and darkness in the depths of the ship, and that is not if they're thrown overboard all together; all potential sapped with nothing left to offer.

To them, the whole ship sinking is no worse. Why would you stick your neck out for people who are so willing to turn against you the moment you're no longer deemed useful anyways?

Kings and Prophets of old saw this as an issue in their time as well; which is often why there is such a social consciousness devoted toward *moral* and *social* rewards, even if not pragmatic ones. You will be awarded a *medal* for giving your resources! Someone will write a nice speech about you! That's nice, eh? Or perhaps you will have your name written in a book of heroes to endure long after you're gone. It may not pay the bills, but it's nice to think about while you're starving! Eventually it caught on that it *wasn't* so good if it couldn't stop you from starving and so things like pensions and compensation and other social contracts were formed wherein it was promised that even if you sacrificed all of your resources, you would *not* be thrown from the ship! You'd even be given a nice bunk and allowed good food to eat! Even if you had nothing to offer! Sometimes they did even more, that even if *you died*, like slipped on a banana peel and went overboard or something, your *family* would be taken care of and not asked to sacrifice any of *their* resources for 20 years or some shit. Or hell, by giving your resources, you could be given rights! Maybe! Good system! Fantastic!

But of course... this is kind of, um, what is politically referred to as a 'wasted expenditure' because come on, all these veterans *already* shot some guys and got shot for us and look it's not like they're gonna be able to go back out there and do it again so *why* are we making sure they're taken care of? Whatever let's just continue putting it off, I'm sure it'll be fine. Speaking of, its kinda weird how nobody signs up for the military anymore, damn, that's nuts, we should offer more *sign-on* packages instead of *post-care* packages, that'll do the trick.

Anyway, I got off track.

. . .

There is a constant balance between the powers that be, because each of them wants to encourage others to spend their resources before they must spend their own; and that goes for eachother as well. It is not that the two men on the far end of this boat do not know they are sinking; they are simply waiting for the other to cave and sacrifice their resources *first*.

And they will do everything they can to encourage others to do exactly this, so they do not have to. So that at the end of it all, it is only they, Captain of the ship, who can make decrees and hand out bribes and ensure, always, their own survival. Ensure, always, that they will not be thrown overboard.

And that is when the first domino of collapse begins. When the ship begins to sink and people know they will be thrown overboard if they ever use up their resources, it only gives *more* incentive to hoarding them instead of using them to keep the thing afloat; because they cannot trust anyone else to keep them there, because someone else just might cave and sacrifice first. So they will hoard, so they can be the last man on a pile of rubble; as if it were a children's game, King of The Hill. May the best man win.

The first of it, perhaps, is that it is easy to avoid such a fate. So long as ideals of honour and self-sacrifice have meaning in your society, with at least some type of equivalence to that of a tangible resource, you will give proper motivation for that self sacrifice even to some of the most hard-hearted of your number. You must never forget this, lest any group you lead suffer the same fate as thousands of others that have risen and fallen before your time.

THE HERO'S CONUNDRUM

$\mathcal{O}$nce upon a time, when watching a documentary on a plane crash in the mountains; I got into a debate with a friend over what the right thing to do was.

We supposed, in this hypothetical, that this plane ferried people of all ages, men and women alike, of varied degrees of health, and crashing to the result of varied degrees of injury (though no one had yet died) so that each survivor had anywhere from a 10%-90% chance of survival each day, decreasing accordingly as the days went on. Furthermore, since the environment was hostile, the only resources they had available were those already on the plane; and since the radio was dead, the only chance of rescue would be if someone made it down the mountain to tell the townsfolk.

My friend argued that the right thing to do was to split the food reserves and medical supplies among the most wounded and needy, so that those who had the lowest chance of surviving would have their chances bolstered to be able to live until rescue.

I, on the other hand, argued that the right thing to do was to preserve the supplies and food stores for those making the trek down the mountain itself; to maximize the chances of them reaching the townsfolk and rescuing the others, even if it meant there were less people alive to rescue.

As the conversation wore on into the night, so too did the premise become more and more abstract. We decided that it was a type of paradox indeed, that the big brave heroes trying to make their way down the mountain were, by the very selflessness they showed in braving the dangers, the LEAST likely to accept any food or aid in favour of giving it to others, however self-defeating that choice was. For if they failed or died in their attempted descent due to a lack of supplies, then everyone else dies too.

It got me to thinking. I remember this comic I read once upon a time: "Crossed", some variation of it, a comic series about hedonistic zombies that you really don't have to read, I promise, but it was worth reading for one section in particular.

On a remote island, the survivors inhabited a lighthouse and the lands surrounding it. The moat surrounding the island made it extremely defensible and safe, but there was not quite enough land on the island itself to grow the food they needed, and they were slowly running out of ammo and medicine. Thus, a plan was concocted: A raffle would be held. Every name on the island would be put into a drum, and the few names pulled would form a group to be sent to the mainland to gather what was needed.

There was an oddity, though. That no raffle was required. There were already enough inhabitants willing to go to the mainland that the team could be assembled immediately. Despite this, the ruling powers insisted that there would be a raffle, no ifs, ands, or buts.

How strange, how odd, to have everything you need and yet choose to subject the unwilling to the horrors of the mainland anyways.

Time after time, tensions rose over this decision; and time after time it was suppressed, until finally, after one close call with the zombies when tensions were at their peak, the administrators burst and told the inhabitants why it was a raffle at all.

"Because the same people willing to go are the exact people we need to stay and defend the island."

Because of course they are.

Of course, if the team took everyone willing, and left only the unwilling, the cowardly, the self-serving, the meek, then the moment any zombie hoard approached the island the defenders would break and run.

Of course, if the team took only the unwilling, they would break and flee to whatever safety they could muster at the first opportunity, never delivering the necessary supplies back to the island proper.

The raffle was the only way they could ever do it. Equal. Fair. So that both groups, the defenders and the retrievers, had cowards and brave folk alike.

This is the core of The Hero's Conundrum; that the same qualities that make someone worth sending also make them worth keeping. That the same person willing to sacrifice themselves is the person you need to live, lest the group lose all heroes and be left with those unwilling to do the same.

Or, as I discussed with an acquaintance some time ago when he posited: *"The most noble thing to do with power is to give it up,"* and I replied: *"The type of person who would give it up is exactly who you'd want to keep it."*

It can go deeper than that even, more abstract, more situational. From a Eugenicist's perspective, the reason we have a society so full of cowards and so lacking the brave is because when the danger comes, the cowards run *away* from the danger while the brave run *toward* it. The brave face the danger, some dying in the process, while all the cowards retain their original numbers; thus not only maintaining the population of cowards, preserving them from harm, but allowing them to propagate and spread their ideals.

From King Solomon's perspective, it was the two women requesting motherhood over a newborn infant, and when Solomon proposed that they simply divide the baby in half by way of his lovely sword, the false mother was ecstatic and the true mother balked, being willing to give up her claim if it meant keeping the baby safe.

From the Leader's perspective, it is the right thing to do to put their strongest in the most precarious of positions, even though losing them would be a far greater blow than losing those weaker.

From the historian's perspective, time and again they see nations divided and consumed by strife and civil war because some few brothers or cousins always insist on waging a bloody conflict, being so willing to drive their nation to ruin if it only means they will be Lord of the heap; and it is clear that the **true** King, the one who SHOULD be King, is the one who relinquished their claim to the throne trying to avoid this mess and preserve their nation.

Of course, that only puts the person *willing* to drive their nation to ruin on the throne, doesn't it?

And here is the conundrum complete. That in some cases, the *most* heroic thing is doing the unheroic thing. To deprive the survivors of aid in order to give it to those making the trek down the mountain. To force the unwilling and cowardly to go with the brave rather than let the defenses of your fortifications waver. To claim the throne and cling to it with all your might so as to keep it from the hands of those who would only bring war and tyranny. To know when to make the terrible choice in order to lead to the greatest outcome.

Recently I saw a video that demonstrates this more pragmatically in the common man; a type of gameshow: 'Double or Take'. The idea goes as follows: You are offered a certain sum of money, which you can either take for yourself, no catch, OR you can double the money offered, the only caveat being that the offer goes to the next person.

So you may get offered $50, and if you take it, you get $50, and if you double it, you get nothing, but the NEXT stranger gets offered $100.

The sum starts at $5, and has gone up to $40, $80, and even over $200 at one point before the offer was too tempting and was taken by the stranger down the line.

In this, the hero's conundrum is demonstrated a bit more clearly; for we can all see, and nigh all agree, that the person who DESERVES the payout is clearly the one willing to give it up in favour of another person getting more. That's the right thing to do. They ought to be rewarded for their benevolence and selflessness. The person who *takes* the money ought to have been the one denied, since this probable selfishness ought to be curbed. And yet in real life this pattern is demonstrated all too frequently. The selfless strive to build for the sake of others, and the selfish destroy for a payout.

There is a videogame that is very good at this sort of showcase. 'Frostpunk', it's called. A city-building sim that takes place in a volcanic winter, with your one and only duty as administrator being to see the city survive and thrive.

Unfortunately it is not so easy as on paper. The balance of resources and expenditures is always tenuous, and it is a common tale that one will have to divert their workforce to gather an emergency reserve of fuel only to then fall behind on other resources, playing a never-ending game of catchup to lay down rails as fast as the train is moving.

There are ways to make it easier, though. You can save energy by decreasing power so that people are always cold but never hypothermic. You can make examples of thieves and plunderers by stripping them and leaving them out in the cold to die for all to see. You can force children to work in your mines. You can institute secret police to keep unions down and organize a state-mandated religion to keep people united and keep rebellions from simmering.

Rebellions brewing because you put their children to work out in the cold, presumably.

You can do many wonderful and terrible things to increase the odds of the city's survival, to push everyone and everything to the brink of monstrousness just to ensure that they are alive to criticize you in the first place.

And at the very end, if you made these choices, the game would ask you a simple question:

"Was it worth it?"

I have heard tell of tales that many Roman Emperors and Kings of old only converted to Christianity outright on their deathbeds, simply because so many of their duties as ruler conflicted with the spiritual tenants of the faith they adored. I have heard, time and again, that 'Great men are rarely good men'. I have heard ring throughout the annals of history how so many rulers did such awful things just to cling to a 'maybe', or a 'perhaps', that if they just do this, this one, last, horrid thing, then their nation and their people will survive.

And maybe it will all be worth it.

I have no doubt that these stories are true in spirit if nothing else, for there are far too many quotes and anecdotes about the difficulties and isolation of leadership to list them all here.

How terrible that what can be right, and what can be necessary, can often be so diametrically opposed. And yet the hero cannot mince between them. There is no room for glory-chasers here. There is no room for those who cannot understand that the greatest sacrifice of all can be your own ethics and morality.

Cherish it while you can.

THE WEST AND THE REST

*T*he other day, whilst rifling through the usual muckabout forums I convince myself I'm learning something from, I stumbled across a comment that read thus verbatim: *"Dude, the American far left is the rest of the worlds centrism."* I know it is verbatim because I had it saved up in another tab for a week so that I could look at it and get angry if I wanted to.

The gent never replied to any of the people lambasting him so I cannot say exactly what he meant beyond generalization, but it doesn't really matter because I'm not replying to him; I am replying to anyone who might hold a similar opinion, to give a wide brushstroke of something they ought to consider before they solidify their opinion as fact.

Therefore, for the sake of clarity, I will assume he meant as people usually do when they make similar claims: that the Progressive party of America's far-left are considered 'normal' elsewhere, that the opinions they have are mild and straight-forward; as opposed to the absurd, regressive, or close-minded views of anything farther right than socialism.

Let it be known that I understand why many people hold this kind of view. If you happen to have been raised in the West, it is very easy to have an idyllic picture of the world, with the idea that violence and savagery are the exception rather than the norm; and are most often brought on by outside influence rather than cultural disagreements.

This view is still categorically wrong, however. And we will get to why in a moment.

As a disclaimer I will tell you now that I am considered quite 'far right' in my views. I tend to favour tradition over progression, militarism over pacifism, and faith over reason. I will try to keep this essay as empirical and unbiased as possible, but if you feel my views would cause me to cherry-pick or that favouritism might cloud my judgement, I do not blame you for dismissing this essay and ask only that you listen to a few of my arguments first before deciding that my arguments are not worth listening to. As a second disclaimer, understand that I am speaking in generalities here. There are some places within any single country that are significantly more progressive than many other regions; nor does every citizen approve of harsh practices. I am mainly speaking in regards to harsh *policy*, rather than how willingly it is carried out or whether everyone always does. I am also not American, if that need be stated.

With that out of the way, let us begin:

To give the initial idea some credit, most of the world's economic, social, or military superpowers do indeed present themselves as progressive and left leaning (to the outside world, at least). This was no more evident than some years ago when North Korea criticized America for its "rape culture", and many progressives used this as ammunition that even a (as of writing) dictatorship could see that America was falling behind yet again in regard to gender equality. Thusly, when media outlets like CNN and New York Times praise Kim Jong Un's sister for her charm and diplomacy during the Winter Olympics, or when the Libertarian Party makes a tweet about how

North Korea has greater freedom than the United States, it is easy to get the impression that even some of the worst the world has to offer still has positive and advanced notions of social progress and equal rights for all, and it is the American-Right who needs to pick up the pace.

Unfortunately, idealistic reader, I must inform you that the nation with a troupe of 'Pleasure Girls' specifically chosen, with some reported to be in their early teens, to serve as prostitutes and muses for the aristocracy (as told from the words of multiple defectors to South Korea) doesn't actually care about gender equality. It must be shocking, I'm sure, to know that when engaging in world politics, politicking is usually done, which mostly just involves how well you can lie and deflect criticism.

It is unfortunate that I can no longer count on both hands how many times I have heard the phrase: *"The rest of the world is laughing at America"* or *"America has lost respect"* when said toward anything even remotely conservative, and it becomes frustrating when said in pangs of loss, lamenting losing the respect of a nation that practices female genital mutilation and foot binding.

After-all, why should you care what someone like Pol Pot would find respectful?

The problem is that the people who say these kinds of things do not look at other cultures and *see* other cultures. They see themselves, their own values and dignities, projected onto other people, convincing themselves that everyone wants the same thing.

But they don't.

This kind of view, to look at our great, wide world with over tens of thousands of different cultures and sub-cultures, with hundreds of thousands of years of history and society making the foundations of our modern world, with a rough one hundred and ninety five different countries, all of whom being born from different actions, circumstances, and opportunity, all of them with their own distinct social dynamics and world view, all of them with their own sense of cultural identity; and to presume that each and every one of them believes exactly as you do, is the height of privilege.

I'm not saying that as a meme. I'm not saying that to 'dunk on the bleeding hearts'. I'm not saying that to get into some petty semantic squabble with your local backpacker. I'm saying it because it's true.

Supposing you, my darling audience, are reading this from the Western World; think not of your continent or an alliance of nations, or even the differences between you and your neighbour. Think of your state, or your province, county, or region. Think only of that, and just how deeply you differ in worldview, politics and social dynamics from someone who resides in a completely separate one. To think that Texas and California, or Alberta and Quebec, or York and Lancaster have the same cultural norms, wants and ideas of progress is ludicrous; and these are sub-cultures that exist within the same country, with the same founding principles of governance and administration. So to extend outward, and earnestly believe that those within cultures completely outside of your core founding philosophy and with a completely different sphere of political, religious, and cultural influence is either willful ignorance or poisonous optimism.

And I don't really care which.

Many of the people who hold this view live in a very protected world. They get their news from Western stations. They consume media either designed by or adapted for Western markets. They talk with foreigners who, dominantly, speak their language rather than the other way around. Even when intentionally delving into foreign markets and forums, they are likely using a search engine that curates their findings to a Western lens of interest. It is no better than someone traveling to another country and staying in a five-star resort and coming out believing they have "seen the culture", instead of the curated caricature of it. There are even separate versions of Wikipedia exclusive to certain countries that tell of different histories, national boundaries, and socially sensitive subjects as seen fit by the censors.

I say this view is protected and privileged because they are only capable of having it in the first place due to a disconnect with the rest of the world at large; seeing it more as a backdrop to the going-ons of their own nation, like an audience to the actor on the stage, rather than separate people living separate lives with separate hopes and dreams, and often living in a much harsher reality.

In nations such as South Sudan, Kenya, Nigeria, and the Philippines, police brutality is less often regarded as law enforcement planting evidence; and often just shooting you in the head without due process.

In Iran, Saudi-Arabia, Somalia, and Yemen, the repression of homosexual rights is often not an issue of being denied same-sex marriage; but usually an issue of avoiding being stoned to death. As a matter of fact, in MOST non-first world countries outside of the West, there is still legal precedent for the death penalty if the judges saw fit; and homosexual murders such as the anti-gay purges in Chechnya often go unpunished.

With the advent of the one-child policy In China, many female infants were either aborted, mistreated, or abandoned outright due to favouritism toward prospective male heirs as reported by census data. In the Democratic Republic of Congo, women are legally subservient to men, with a married woman requiring her husband's permission to open a bank account, accept a job, obtain a commercial license, or rent or sell real estate. In India, 35,493 dowry deaths (a practice of murdering your wife as a protest for insufficient dowry) were reported across the country by the Minister of State between the years 2017 and 2021, and still account for a rough 40-50% of all female homicides annually. All the worse that these murders are often done through immolation via kerosene, and can feasibly be a cooking accident, resulting in only a rough 30% of all suspicious deaths actually being brought before a court and gaining a conviction. I am confident in stating that the West's ideas of female prosperity and comfort is not high on the abusers' list of priorities.

Whilst in the West, a violation of your religious rights includes forced overlaps between religious taboo and economic or social obligation (such as a Christian being fined for not baking a cake for a gay wedding). In Burma, it includes the non-Buddhist minority being denied building permits, freedom to hold church and temple services, and being denied citizenship. Eritrea follows a similar pattern; recognizing only four religions, three of them being different sects of the one major religion, and all the rest being subject to punitive measures ranging from being denied congregation to hard labor for conscientious objection. In Uzbekistan they often skip all that and just arbitrarily label certain religious denominations as extremists so to be legally justified in raiding their places of worship, burning their books, arresting the practitioners, and holding them in inhumane conditions as reported by the Human Rights Watch.

On August 28th, 1963, Dr. Martin Luther King Jr. gave his famous *"I Have A Dream"* speech; with his campaign and civil rights activism paving the way for equal, if tenuous, race relations in the USA. In contrast, a wave of government sanctioned ethnic cleansing against Rohingya Muslims, with thousands killed, villages burned, and every man, woman, and child within them being executed was reported in Myanmar as early as 2017. But even this is a step above the Turkish occupation of Northern Syria, where up to 300,000 Kurds, Christians, and Yazidis were either displaced or executed. I would like to give dates as to when this took place, but I can't, because as of the writing of this document in March 2023, it is still ongoing. This does not include the cultural cleansing of Muslims and Tamil in Sri Lanka, the killing of hundreds of ethnic Uzbeks in Kyrgyzstan during race-riots, the genocide of the Darfur peoples in Western Sudan, the ethnic cleansing of Syrian Christians, and constant conflict displacing multiple ethnic groups all throughout central Africa; and these are only notable events within the last two decades, saying nothing of the past sixty years.

These are just to make an example of the more horrid cases of barbarism and bigotry; rather than touching on the relatively more moderate ideas of societies that follow rigid traditionalist gender roles, religious law and custom, punitive measures, and even soft caste systems, along with doubtless many other things that would make my far-left friends faint, up to and including the active and persistent practice of slavery that is still going on in countries such as Burundi, the Central African Republic, Bangladesh, and Cambodia. Among others. Many others.

This is why the idea of America, or any Western country for that matter, 'losing respect in the world' has always been a spot for condescension for me since it supposes from the get-go that every other country and culture in the world has the exact same idea of 'respect' as you do.

They do not.

I am reminded of this excellent graphic novel I once read: 'WAR IS BORING' by David Axe, a conflict photographer and journalist, wherein he describes an experience of sitting in a Café in a war-torn part of the world, editing his works as he sipped his pop, when there was suddenly a loud crash and a boom. Just down the street a bomb had hit a building, causing it to crumble to the ground as shockwaves rent the hair from people's faces and clothes from their backs, raining dust down in every crevice as the owner of the café ran out the front door, shook his fist at the sky, and screamed expletives about "**THOSE BASTARDS!**" until he was red in the face.

Before calmly turning, addressing David, and asking *"By the way, did you want a refill on that coke?"*

It is not a matter of left versus right thinking or a matter for academics to discuss the merits of progress. In many of these areas I named, this is simply the way it is, and the most frequent way change occurs is through civil conflict and unrest. Riots. Terrorism. Coups. And not always a positive change either; as in many such conflicts of the last fifty years, leaps in progress and equal rights between sexes or races or religions was annulled. This is not political allegiance or wars of ideology. For many, this is life.

I find it ironic then, that so many of these countries with so much turmoil and traditionalist attitudes are so patriotic in their fervor. Many of them genuinely, truly, love their country, despite its faults; whilst the West will actively suppress any Nationalistic sentiment with all the force that shame and guilt can provide. It is ironic that a country which may regularly shed the blood of its dissidents feels so proud, while the West, for all its progressivism and pushes for equality and nurturing, is ashamed of it.

In getting this far into my essay, you may be thinking that I am unaware of the effects western imperialism and aggressive trade has often had in these countries, but that is not so. The west has had its fair share of blood; from banana republics to economic leverages that enforce practices of slavery and serfdom. *My* problem is that it is often not *these* aspects being criticized; but rather, issues on the Homefront. Not doing enough for minority representation or not acting to ensure fair treatment among the poor, and administrations and businesses bow down and plead to make amends all while continuing their horrid practices overseas and in less developed countries.

It is all well and good for people to upset with Coca-Cola's potential abuse of black employees, but it is not often I see people rage at them over being accused of funding paramilitaries to assassinate union leaders in Columbia. Almost as if businesses and administrations commit and broadcast lighter infractions so that the heavier and worse ones remain unnoticed. Funny, that. Personally I just wish it wasn't so successful.

Believe me, I am well aware of the wrongs done by the west, and I will gladly run them through the muck over it another time. But this essay isn't about that. Nor is it comparing the thinking of peace-time mindsets against war-time mindsets, or mindsets in times of security against times of uncertainty. For the sake of clarity I am only focusing on one issue at a time, and right now I am trying to call into the spotlight the cultural values that often leads to these laws, conflicts, and abuses to begin with. If you wish for more Western hate instead, look elsewhere. It is not as if it is hard to find.

. . .

Some might rightly point out that, especially in regard to certain regions of Africa or the Middle East, destabilization and regression was fueled in part by a more Imperialist West. But even though this is true; if some shadowy government organization left a box of guns on your doorstep, it is still up to you to use them. Whatever internal political struggles, shadowy dealings, and economic pressures forced China to intern certain religious denominations in concentration camps, it is still the inner cultural monologues that allow it to take place to begin with. The value one places on any given subject, and what their end goals are, and what methods they believe are acceptable to attain them.

Perhaps there is no greater indication of the cultural rift between the West and elsewhere than with international views on Adolf Hitler. In the West, he is, obviously, demonized and is used as an example of a monstrous individual and the dangers of authoritarianism and tyranny. In most Western countries it is illegal to even register as a National-Socialist party; any groups espousing anything close to Nazi rhetoric are purged and broken up; and the sheer idea of nationalism blooming in any form across the Western European world is enough to cause most politicians to cringe.

But it isn't like this everywhere. In fact, it isn't like this in most places at all.

On September 30th, 2016, Philippine President Rodrigo Duterte was quoted as saying:

"Hitler massacred 3 million Jews [sic]. Now there are 3 million drug addicts [in the Philippines].... I'd be happy to slaughter them!"

and contrary to all Western sensibility; this seems to have only bolstered his popularity, with him being considered a man who speaks his mind and gets things done.

In 2003, Robert Mugabe, President of Zimbabwe at the time, was quoted in a speech saying:

"I am still the Hitler of [this] time. This Hitler has only one objective: justice for his people, sovereignty for his people, recognition of the independence of his people and their rights over their resources. If that is Hitler, then let me be Hitler tenfold. Ten times, that is what we stand for"

with, yet again, only an increase in popularity outside of the West.

In Indonesia, the first and second President both held Hitler and the Third Reich in high regard, with the first President Sukarno using the Third Reich as a prime example of independence, nationalism, and liberation during his resistance of Dutch administration; and the second President Suharto using it as a model for his highly centralized 'New Order'. An anonymous professor of History at Gadjah Mada University in Yogyakarta explained it as:

"They see Hitler as a revolutionary, similar to Che Guevara, not as someone responsible for the death of millions of Jews."

It should surprise nobody that Hitler is relatively popular in most middle eastern and Muslim dominated nations, including Turkey, Egypt, and Pakistan, for a variety of reasons varying from troubled histories with the allied powers to religious differences with Jews to even more positive views of authoritarianism.

In Japan, there is an entire aesthetic devoted to Nazi Samurai for surely obvious reasons. In Thailand, Nazi imagery and cosplay is often considered hip. In India, the name Hitler and associations with the Third Reich are put to use to curate eye-grabbing and chic products. In many Latin American nations, Falangist Sympathy retains a relatively minor, but steady hold. And finally, 'Afro-Fascism' describes a phenomenon of African leaders replicating themselves after Fascist Italy or the Third Reich.

I will mention once again that none of this applies to *every* part of a singular country or people. Sweeping generalizations are not only *bad*, but often *incorrect*. I am only mentioning **patterns**, *not* universal truths, and I mention them because I need you to understand that different views on the same subject can lead to radically different perspectives on how it is interpreted. Most people do not think as you do, and their motivations and reasonings, when boiled down to the roots as to why, can seem wildly alien.

When you think of Culture, what pops into your head? Food, perhaps. That's a common one. Certain architecture on old buildings if you're a geek. Religious ceremonies. Fashion. It might be harder to think of anything deeper; mostly because these things I just named are the most easily noticeable or commercialized. It is difficult to think of anything more because so many cultural aspects are so engrained that they are invisible to us, which is why, if you were raised in the West in the early 2000's, you might have a voice in your head that automatically pings *"White people have no culture."* And why wouldn't it? English food is notoriously bland and what else is there?

People rarely consider things like the concept of 'modesty' or 'beauty' to be cultural, but they are. Same with how children ought to be raised. How inheritance is passed on and who gets it. Which animals are food, and which are friends. The relationships between boss and subordinate. Moral crimes. The processes of dating and marriage. What 'justice' is. Incentives to work. What a leader's responsibilities are. Behaviour on versus off the clock. How groups are oriented and make decisions. What counts as clean versus dirty. How you feel about the dependent and less fortunate. Disease theory. Your first approaches to problem solving. What it means to "move up in the world" and who is even capable of doing so. How you are to treat family, friends, teachers, the elderly, your co-workers, and strangers by default. What it means for someone to be insane. Styles of storytelling. When someone becomes your 'friend' and what an appropriate way to interact with them is. Who "you" are and what defines you. Body language. What characterizes something to be logical versus illogical. Appropriate emotional control. Appropriate conversation and modes of treatment between your varied social circle. What it means for something to be in the past and in the future. Taboos. Whether time is seen as an active or passive resource.

Whether you are competitive or cooperative by default. What a normal amount of social interaction is and who you have it with. What it means to be a child, teenager, or adult. One's relationship to authority figures. What counts as good manners. What it means for something to be "fair" and how it relates to the relationship between those deciding on it. One's relationship to death, honour, integrity, the gods, your ancestors, or nature. What an appropriate amount of affection or physical contact is between friends, family, or lovers. What appropriate standards, policies, and procedures are for things ranging from legal work to setting up get-togethers with friends. The very way your grammar functions.

Let the record show that these too are only the broad strokes. These are the most basic considerations of what it means to come from a different culture and way of thinking, because it takes nothing about how these things relate to eachother, relate to circumstances such as places or times or events, or even sub-cultures of whether you are perceiving all of this as a man or a woman, or from the younger generation or the older, or as a blue collar versus white collar worker, or your schooling, or where you live, or your income level, or your political and religious views; nigh all of which, all those slivers of separate views on the same subject, being unique and important to your sub-group and no other.

It sounds so strange to think that even something as objective seeming as disease control and waste management can mean different things in different cultures, but the truth is that the only reason you have not seen it in this light previously is because your cultural standards are so engrained in you, with your raising and rearing, nature and nurture, that any deviation you held from the common standard WAS deviation from 'the norm'; and if someone had a different view by default then they either obviously must be wrong or must be mad.

To take this to its extreme, in India, the Ganges river suffers from pollution levels unseen in most any other habited region on the planet and yet it remains a problem that people will cleanse themselves in it or use its water for funeral or medicinal rituals. They do this because it is a holy site. To many in the West, this seems contradictory; as in our cultural view, holy sites must be kept clean of filth at all times in order to maintain their purity, but in their cultural view, it is *because* it is holy that it *cannot* be made dirty. Yet this kind of mindset never even crosses our minds; it sounds ridiculous, as even those who intentionally dirty holy sites in the West do so with the cultural rearing that they are breaking a taboo and intentionally disrespecting tradition. To see how many of them treat the Ganges would cause you to second-guess its status, that perhaps they do not respect it as much as you've been led to believe. But that's wrong. That, unto itself, is part of your cultural rearing. They just view 'holiness' differently. Even when one deviates from cultural norms, they still do so at the outset of what those norms were to begin with; things ingrained so deep that they are never considered *cultural* to begin with. They just... **are.**

In his book *"Decline of The West"*, Oswald Spengler defines Western culture as stemming from Celtic-Germanic tribal roots, its prime symbol being 'Boundless Space' represented by sub-type symbols of eternity (such as circles, plants with ever spanning roots, and horizons appearing frequently in art and religious media), with meaning influenced by Faustian dialectic which is characterized as having strong feelings toward the infinite (Think: Our media depictions of Empire, the soul, and scientific discovery) and who's greatest tragedy is striving for what cannot be attained (Think: Great Gatsby, Romeo and Juliet, and Titanic). The West's great battles are often depictions of one degree of limitlessness balanced against another (such as the trading of a soul for wealth or knowledge, the brilliant metaphorical man [nature, collective, art, etc] vs the enduring metaphorical machine [industry, tyranny, a colourless world, etc], and duels between heroes of eternal legend against immortal gods).

At the top of the cultural pyramid is the "Will-to-Power"; often expressed by the symbolic importance of exploration, infinitesimal calculus, music, heliocentrism, the Inquisition/Global Proselytism, and energy and entropy. Western cultural nuances often stem from root mindsets of overcoming obstacles (rather than diverting them) with purposeful (rather than passive) action, a religion requiring that others be converted, a science focused on force and physics, and art focused on perspective and direction; all with the ultimate goal of changing the world.

Even something as small seeming as parents urging their children to pull themselves up by the bootstraps and walk into a workplace to demand an interview, whilst children try to explain the radically shifting world and the need to adapt, can be traced back to these roots.

Western 'needs' include: Confession, Autobiography, Gothic Architecture, Skyscrapers, Globalization, and Perpetual Motion. These too, the needs for the truth to be known, for beauty and freedom, and world-wide ripple effects can be found in the roots of Western culture.

And even these are broad strokes. Even with all of this, a Frenchman is still going to see war far differently than an American.

This is just the West. This is the very tip of the iceberg of Western culture, with absolutely zero input as to the subcultures that make up the whole of it, giving their own spin and view and perspective on each of these principles.

I hope you see what I meant now, when I talked about how staggering differences of cultural nuance could be between those within the same country, let alone your neighboring country. The cultural differences that separate gulfs between someone in one section of the Western sphere and one in the East can, when looked at closely, appear insurmountable. THIS is what people mean when they shout, with righteous fury and indignation, *"You could never understand!"*

That does not mean that we cannot get along, though. Or *have* understanding even against such a pessimistic view.

. . .

I remember once, when I was very young, watching a documentary featuring a Saudi Prince; and after a fun day of falconry in the desert, he sets up a rest-spot and invites the camera crew to sit with him. They do, and he shows them this treat he likes; it is a roasted marshmallow squished between two Ma'amul shortbreads, and he smiles at the camera and remarks that he calls it a desert cookie, and that he felt that those in the West and himself were not so different, because he heard we enjoyed sweets too.

And he was right. I do have quite the sweet tooth. I would have loved to show him a S'more.

There is 1,800 year old graffiti of dicks and bathroom poetry carved into the walls of Pompeii by the Roman citizens passing by.

The oldest recorded name for a cat dates from Ancient Egypt, and its translation means "Sweetie."

There are letters from the Song Dynasty of China where Zen Buddhists ribbed one another, and then mocking eachother further when they got offended.

There is a two-millennium old Peruvian mummy whose hair samples told us he drank too much corn beer.

There are strips of softened birch bark, made eight hundred years ago, for a young boy named Onfim of Novgorod to write on, and when he finished his language lessons, he used them to draw himself as a knight on a horse.

There are statues of women and chambermaids, from across dozens of countries, that are hundreds and thousands of years old, who's painted shell over their cleavage has been wiped away, or who's bronze breasts have been shined to gold, because of how many people rubbed them over the years.

Because no matter our cultures and no matter what divides us, there will always be more that makes us similar. We all fight, we all drink, we all make love, we all dream, and we all laugh at obscene humor and delight in fantasies. People have always just been people; as they are, even now.

We really can all be friends, if we try. Wars are becoming rarer and modern relations incentivize trade over militarization any day of the week. Peace and harmony can be achieved with the right incentives and respect.

I am only trying to get across the same point I had since the very beginning; that you must be aware that your idea of what incentives and respect are, are vastly different from another's. To either demonize *or* patronize will miss the point. This is a great big world, and there is enough space for all of us, if only we try to understand.

THE OBSOLESCENCE OF
DECISIVE EVIDENCE

I have seen pornography of a certain speaker for the House of Representatives. In particular it was a video of her giving a handjob. Not exactly enthralling, but we're not here to discuss taste.

The video was a fake, of course. As were the videos featuring certain actresses, singers, and one former president.

As far as I'm aware, these people have never done porn. And certainly not with closeups.

As a matter of fact, there's a *lot* of videos and pictures out there of women doing porn, with a grand portion of them never actually participating; and some of them not existing at all. Instead, they're usually made with a program dubbed 'FakeApp', where, with input of the subject's face, still images or  otherwise, the A.I is then 'trained' to copy that face; contours, head-turns, face-tilts and all, onto whatever body you put it on as believably as possibly.

This kind of application, both the program and the act itself, are often referred to as a 'Deepfake'.

Deepfakes need not only be for people, of course. Objects, scenarios, environments, voices, text-messages; so long as something has been uploaded to the internet, it counts; the purpose being in the name: to make a convincing fake. Usually for the sake of satire or eroticism.

Usually.

More damaging, they are a symptom of what I've heard described as a *"Post-Truth Society."*

Fake texts are the most common one. Programs for it are so prolific that you can access most of them right through your browser, creating any fake conversation required for any operating system and even plenty of social media sites, some of which go so in-depth that it can mirror the functions of the site itself; votes, shares, comments, the works.

Not that you even have to go that far. Depending on your browser, playing around with the 'Inspect Element' feature will allow you to change pictures/texts/numbers regardless. Only for you, of course; it doesn't change what the site or text actually shows, only how you, personally, see it. But that wouldn't stop anyone from saving the edits and presenting them as authentic elsewhere. That's why techies tell you to never trust a screenshot and always find the source.

Wombo is a popular one too. Also called 'Wombo.ai', it's a Canadian image manipulation mobile app developed by Ben-Zion Benkhin and his team for the iOS and Android. Released in 2021, it uses a provided selfie to create a deepfake of a person grooving and lip-syncing to one of various songs. The selfie need not be yours either. Some funny videos I've seen made with it include the likes of former President Donald Trump, Chris-Chan, and Vladimir Lenin; so even still-images can be digitally altered to make it look like they're moving and speaking.

Pixilated images are no longer safe either. The PULSE (Photo Upsampling via Latent Space Exploration) system is an A.I that can create hyper-realistic faces and scenery from deeply pixilated pictures. Though the scenes and faces created are currently falsified and the system as a whole is considered a work-in-progress, programmers are attempting to refine it to be as true-to-life as possible, for all the advances in astronomy, medicine, and archeology that it can provide. That being said, its utility in discovering the identities of would-be resistance fighters at the behest of tyrannical governments, or poachers and pirates to deduce the locations of their next ill-gotten gains, is not lost on me.

Even voices can be faked with only a few lines of existing dialogue. Lyrebird, a voice-synthesizing software bought by Descript, can clone the voice and cadence of any individual with voice samples from past interviews, and some of the best boast the ability to synthesize a nearly identical voice from only a few lines of dialogue. Though this software is far from perfect, and Descript's stated intentions are to use it for easy text-to-voice podcast/script recordings, it is certainly disquieting to know that you can be made to potentially say anything; confessions, compromising statements, or even passwords, provided a recording of you saying a sentence or two can be found.

It goes even further, with apps like DeepSwap meshing your face and body over actors and models in recorded performances. Or StyleGAN which can create lifelike portraits of people that don't exist. Or the rising power of special effects and its ability to simulate worlds and environments that aren't real.

None of this is actually a warning against the dangers of shoddy tech-security either (though that in itself is a subject worth discussing, with Jan Krissler, a White-Hat hacker based in Germany, revealing at the annual Chaos Communication Congress that he was able to re-create the fingerprints of the standing German Defense Minister using only high-resolution photographs. For posterity, this is the same Jan Krissler who overcame Apple's thumbprint verification within 24 hours of the iPhone 5S release). Rather, it's just to bring light onto the fact that… well things seem rather easy to fake, don't they?

It is worth noting, of course, that none of these systems are perfect. In a lot of media there is a ton of metadata that we cannot perceive without going into the guts of the thing. This metadata could provide a level of authenticity that few deepfakes could match (for now, anyways…). A proposed solution is that tech companies can provide tools to make finding meta-data simpler, especially as we progress in technological literacy, by including indelible and imperceptible "watermarks" into the media, to allow for it to be authenticated (for a price). Though even this would one day be susceptible to the same fakery we are trying to prevent…

The more realistic scenario would be akin to a state-run 'archive of truth'. Just as the internet archive maintains a history of the web, states may choose to maintain an archive of a selection of, or all, media and internet content. The advantage of this is clear, as it would allow for appeals to the archive to settle any disputes. On the other hand this would also effectively grant individual states or alliances the power to dictate truths unilaterally. 1984 indeed.

I would be amiss to not mention blockchains and "NFT's" despite the infamy they have attained. In a sense, a blockchain is a ledger into which you could enter data, and which would be very difficult to try to alter afterwards.

And even in the present day where few of these are applicable to media-authenticity, errors already exist in each of the deepfake applications, and some of the crappier, free versions are so shoddy you can tell at a glance that it's not the real deal. But it's improving. The precedent is there. And technology only improves over time. There are some programs that, with time and resources put into it, can be *startlingly* convincing. And while it is true that deep dives into the metadata itself can often prove whether texts or pictures or what-have-you are the genuine articles... that can take time and cross-references and big words.

While rumor spreads fast.

The court of public opinion is not known for its patience.

If you go back throughout history and do some research as to the method of crime-solving and police-work, you will quickly find that it was, frankly, not very good. It was not very good because they didn't have all the methods of tracking and obtaining evidence that we have today. The blood of a pig and the blood of a man splatter the same in the butcher's shop, the hand-print on the wall was nothing more than a smudge because you couldn't get fingerprints off it yet, and surveillance systems essentially amounted to someone's grandmother looking out the window. Which means that the only way to catch a criminal was to judge the profile of their character and reputation before making sure they didn't have an alibi, getting a confession, or catching them red-handed.

Things improved with the development of D.N.A and sample analysis, along with the creation of surveillance technology, and just recently I heard a report of police tracking down a suspect based on a shirt they were wearing, what small shop they bought it from, and cross-referenced the subject's appearance with the list of buyers. All of this, though imperfect, goes a long way toward confirming guilt or innocence.

And yet... We seem to be sort of tunneling back, now. There have already been spats in online communities and forums, big-name creators being accused of X or Y only to find that record and testimony had been falsified, or people dogpiling on a user for proofs that later turned out to be edited. Not that such a thing being proven stopped people from trying to ruin their lives.

In the minds of some, accusation is a form of evidence unto itself.

And the accusations are only going to be more and more finely edited as time goes on, and even time and place will no longer matter. The average adult spends a rough seven hours of their day online, and in some nations that average only climbs higher and higher. That is a lot of time to be a suspect.

I wonder how many lives will be ruined then. How many women will lose their profession or relationships because fake porn surfaced somewhere, created by a jilted suitor. How many men will be thrown into prison because of edited footage to make them look like an exhibitionist. How many people will have to deal with attempts at blackmail; not for anything they did, but for what the accuser could it make it *look* like they're doing.

I wonder how long this will all go on, how many people it will harm in its wake until we, as a society, do away with such technological proofs all together. Until we go right back around to character. And confession. And being caught red-handed.

I HAVE A BONE TO PICK WITH THE SCIENTIFIC COMMUNITY.

*N*ot some insolent vendetta, mind you. Not some angry fist-shaking at some scientist I disagree with. Not because of any fringe theories they refute or even my own occult interests which they often deride. Nor is it a critique of the academic 'fandom', though they too play a part in this.

This is not personal, but it must be said all the same.

There are those among this crowd, both the academics and their fans, who would claim that since I myself am not a scientist, then I shouldn't presume to speak on this matter; to which I respond that if we all kept silent about things which we were not masters of, then some people could only talk about one subject and most couldn't talk about anything at all; or I would say that I'm not a helicopter pilot and yet I know it shouldn't land in a tree. Whichever sounds more poetic by the end of this.

With all that said, let it be known that I too am a fan of science. I consider myself an academic in case you couldn't tell by my vast ego in publishing works entirely made up of my opinions. I benefit from medicine and modern engineering, I enjoy my food cold, I like coffee whilst living outside of the coffee belt, and I am not forced to chisel this essay into limestone. All of these things are possible through scientific advancement. Great job, lads.

My critique, then, is not over the profession itself. Not entirely. Rather, It is on the romantic mantle of those within it, and those who endorse it. Because above all else, 'science' rarely pays very well. Much like being a teacher, or a librarian, or a fireman, these kinds of cerebral professions (except the last one, sorry himbos) are seen more as a point of virtue. They accept the low pay and long hours for the pursuit of truth and the protection of the community. In this, one could argue that the true wage of the academic is the trust the public puts in them. All one need do is *disagree* with an academic, or be called out by one, to become the subject of mockery and ridicule. This is why most any inane or silly action can be handwaved as 'for research'; it is why there is an influx of amateurs conducting 'social experiments' to dodge accountability for their shitty behaviour; and it is why many politicians often flank themselves with rows of scientists before giving any grand speech that effects public interest.

People often trust academics, as they should. Because the academic fandom does have one thing right, in that between trusting an amateur or a professional, you ought to trust the professional. But this kind of wage leads to a type of elevation of status; where one is BEYOND disagreement, BEYOND criticism. Scientists and their ilk are often seen less as humans working a job and more as paragons of virtue and enlightenment, a living incarnation of absolute progress.

Which, no matter how positive, is still a measure of dehumanization.

. . .

This, then, is the core of my critique. Something that many members of the fandom, bureaucrats, and even celebrity scientists themselves often forget.

They are just people.

Not people of particular wisdom and virtue, though I'm sure some of them are.

They are just people.

Just as bias, just as arrogant, just as flawed as you or I.

They are no more infallible, no more incorruptible, than a professional in any other field, an expert in any other profession. Just as a Judge tends to rule more harshly before lunch, and more leniently after. Just as police officers have higher rates of domestic violence. Just as the Vatican has historically covered up abuse.

So too are academics *just* people.

 We often think of scientists as the ones leading the way, the ones carrying the blazing torch of truth to light our way in the dark; the media trope of the 'Ignored Expert', the lone person who knows the sky is falling and how to handle it whilst everyone else squabbles over petty issues is almost always a scientist. Yet in history, the expert being ignored is often a victim, not to an ignorant public or an unwavering King, but of their own peers.

John Snow, often called the grandfather of Epidemiology for his work in diagnosing the cause of cholera outbreaks in London, was himself a skeptic of Miasma-Theory; the dominant medical theory at the time that disease was spread, as the name suggests, through a pungent miasma. He believed, as his research would eventually prove correct, that illnesses could be traced to specific contaminants, such as fecal matter in water. Today recognized as the basis of Germ-Theory.

But most of his opponents to this bold new theory were not the common man. John Snow was, indeed, a doctor. People trusted him when he told them to get their water from elsewhere. No, it was his own colleagues and those on the Health Commission who dismissed the grand portion of his findings; stating that it surely *was* a miasma hanging around the pump, with the pump itself just being in an unfortunate location.

It wasn't until much later, after Snow's report (circa 1854) was joined by numerous others, that Germ-Theory was professionally considered. By the end of the decade.

The story of Ignaz Semmelweis is similar, who, in his efforts to reduce Childbed Fever, found that most deaths were caused when doctors performed surgeries and autopsies on one patient before going directly to assist in the childbirth of another, without sanitizing their hands or equipment. He became a proponent for handwashing, a theory utterly rejected by his contemporaries, who would either twist his findings or simply dismiss him all together, mocking his ideas in the press.

He was ridiculed to such an extent that he developed a nervous depression, lashing out at critics and peers and eventually being committed to an insane asylum where he died, weeks later, from infection. Ironic.

His death was passed over with little attention, and not even addressed by the association for which he dedicated his life's work. Even after his successor was appointed, and death rates increased sixfold following the dismissal of his practices, there was neither inquiries, nor protest, from his peers. It was only twenty years following his death that his guidelines were put into common practice, with the help of Louis Pasteur's cementing of Germ-Theory.

In modern psychology, it is theorized that many doctors and scientists of his day were especially rejective of his theory because, if they accepted it, it would mean that they were regularly killing their own patients.

Indeed, his ideas were dismissed so absolutely that his very name became its own symptom: "The Semmelweis Reflex", referring to behaviour characterized by a reflexive rejection of new knowledge because it contradicts with entrenched norms and traditions.

It is counter-intuitive to think so, but scientists are traditionalists by nature. Groundbreaking innovations and new discoveries are made, not by the status quo, but of break-away theories. Scientists, by instinct, are forced to tow a line. Their work is built off of previously set foundations. Their studies entrenched in the evidence their forefathers found, as if knowledge grows like branches from the trunk of a tree; and if a branch is ingrown or gnarled then it must be cut and tended so that a new theory springs forth from the same foundation, rather than each fact being a tree unto itself.

Scientists of Snow's day didn't reject Germ-Theory because they were angry at his dashing looks or because they really liked killing the poor, but because they were working off of previously endorsed and proven theories of the past. They believed, with all certainty, that they were correct. It was John Snow that was the crackpot.

But of course, I am told, that this just happened in the old days. It's not like it is *now* where these kinds of discoveries are taken very seriously because we've *learned* from our past sins.

But we haven't.

The idea of Plate Tectonics was first developed by Alfred Wegener in 1912 and was not considered mainstream until 1966. Theories of Behavoural Economics were proposed as early as the 1700's and yet were not considered model for business practice until 2002, mostly due to a reluctance to accept psychology as a true discipline. 'Bell's Theorem', the idea that quantum physics predicted instant action at a distance, was first proposed by John Bell in 1964 and was largely dismissed by his academic fellows, including Albert Einstein himself who mocked it as "Spooky Action". It wasn't until 1972 when the experiment was even considered and performed by John Clauser and Stuart Freedman that it was proven actually significant. The discipline of Experimental Psychology was first categorized for academic research in 1879 by Willhelm Wundt (or circa 1890's with Psychoanalysis by Sigmund Freud depending on who you ask) and yet even to this day, debate rages on about whether psychology is a 'true' science, deserving of respect or even consideration by its more 'hard science' oriented peers.

We do not know what radical idea is being proposed today, but there is surely one, and it will be looked back on with shame and remorse that it was not discovered sooner, not for a lack of equipment or specialty, but simply for a lack of interest. A pure dismissal based on the fallacy of arguing from incredulity, that it *sounds* mad and so *cannot* be true.

Let it be known that I am not encouraging instant acceptance of all fringe theories. Most of them are wrong. Dead in the water. Replacing a man's entire nervous system with ground-up cereal is surely a fringe procedure but that does not make it correct just because it's anti-mainstream like some kind of infohazard hipster. What I am instead pointing out is that the sphere of academia, rather than being governed by some idealistic mix of progress and reason alone, is composed of human beings, with vested opinions, prejudices, and orthodoxies at no less a rate than any other sphere, be it political or religious.

Make no mistake. Science does have its heresies.

James D. Watson is an American molecular biologist, geneticist, and zoologist who's claim to fame is the co-authorship of the academic paper that proposed the double-helix structure of the DNA molecule. For this discovery, he, along with his co-researchers, were awarded a Nobel Prize. He went on to serve as director of Cold Spring Harbor Laboratory (CSHL) and succeeded in greatly expanding its level of funding and research, resulting in many breakthroughs in the study of cancer along with making it a world-leading research center in molecular biology.

For his many accomplishments and good works, he has been given numerous honours, including: the Albert Lasker Award for Basic Medical Research, the Membership of the National Academy of Sciences, the John J. Carty Award, being sworn in as a Foreign Member of the Royal Society, gaining an EMBO Membership, a Copley Medal, and a Lomonosov Gold Medal.

Not that any of these matter anymore, because he also stated, off the record, that he is of the opinion that there is a genetic link between one's race and intelligence.

Because of these rather gross remarks, the lab he served for 40 years revoked all honours and awards they previously bestowed to him. He later reiterated his opinions in a PBS documentary and the CSHL board was shocked to find that humiliating someone and forcing them into retirement didn't actually change their opinions, so they just severed all ties with him instead.

"Dr. Watson's statements are reprehensible, unsupported by science, and in no way represent the views of CSHL, its trustees, faculty, staff, or students. The laboratory condemns the misuse of science to justify prejudice." - "The statements he made in the [PBS] documentary are completely and utterly incompatible with our mission, values, and policies, and require the severing of any remaining vestiges of his involvement," Simons and Stillman said.

To the credit of CSHL, they did say they appreciated his many decades of dedicated service, and it was purely a matter of his abhorrent opinions that they could no longer allow him his honours (which, to reiterate, had nothing to do with his personal views) or work with him after he spent the better part of his life improving their facilities and helping to study and treat cancer.

How convenient.

I wonder if they utilize the resources his administration provided with the same guilty looks as many scientists do today knowing they're working off of Nazi research. You know, the same Nazi scientists who were given full clemency for all their crimes against humanity if they just came and worked for the good guys instead.

This kind of thing leaves a bad taste in my mouth. It's the same feeling I get when I read of yet another product, another universe, another IP based off the works of H.P. Lovecraft, and in the same breath they use to try to sell their product based off his works, they decry him and throw him into the muck for his unsavoury social views.

Because as it happens, people are more than happy to poach and profit from your work, so long as they can grandstand about what a good person they are while they do it.

James Watson went on to suffer financial troubles due to no longer being openly employable in his academic field, go figure, and was forced to auction off his hard-won Nobel Prize to make ends meet, along with the notes for his Nobel acceptance speech, and the manuscript for the lecture that he gave the day after he received the medal (Though, in an act of supreme kindness and charity, the winner of the auction, Alisher Usmanov, returned the medal to Watson under the promise that a portion of the proceeds would go to further charities for cancer research).

Regardless of your views on his idea of race and intelligence, it is still clear proof that there is both a political and social bias in the academic field; where holding unsavoury views, even if they have nothing to do with your work, could still get you exiled, and your work sullied.

If you require yet more proof of political presence in Academia, I'd encourage you to ask Bruce Aylward, Senior Advisor to the World Health Organization (abbreviated as WHO) how he feels about Taiwan gaining WHO membership and see how fast he hangs up on you like he did to RTHK reporter Yvonne Tong, insisting that they had already discussed "China". (For those not in the know, China considers Taiwan part of its sovereign territory. Taiwan disagrees. The WHO too regards Taiwan as part of Chinese territory and seems to refuse to acknowledge any cultural or political difference between them, much to the despair of the Taiwanese. This is the same WHO that agreed with Chinese Health preliminary investigations that the Coronavirus was non-transmissible from human to human.

The WHO's seeming deference to China, its policies, and the frankly embarrassing amount of praise it lavishes on them has been heavily criticized since the start of the pandemic, and has led to a much greater degree of scrutiny over its motives for doing so. The German broadcasting station "Deutsche Welle" has interviewed experts who speculate that the vast amount of economic might China holds in its grasp may well be a tempting target to an organization that relies so heavily on donations and dues from member-states. All such cases seemingly suggesting that academic virtue might not always be at the forefront of their minds...)

On the opposing end, there are those I've related this story to (the James Watson one) who told me that while they don't necessarily agree with the board's decision, still believe Watson wouldn't have been a good fit to stay in his profession *anyways*; since he could have been made bias by his views and influenced his findings thereby, but I do not agree.

I do not believe his opinions would influence his work in the same way that a chef not liking the taste of fish wouldn't necessitate their intentionally spoiling it when cooking it for others. Despite Watson's rather, um... *odd* views, his works doubtless went to furthering and bettering humanity as a whole; not only through his professional life, but also in charities he took part in and the signing of the Humanist Manifesto. He has always *seemed* well meaning, even in his views on race, stating that he did not mean to give vent or fuel to racist ideas and was simply trying to acknowledge what he saw as a fact.

Furthermore, even if his views *did* colour his work, wouldn't that just prove my point anyways? That an academic, no matter their honours and works, is still just a human being, prone to human bias that can influence them for better or worse? Would that *still* not apply to everyone?

Finally, suppose he had the opposite view. Suppose he viewed Africans as intellectually superior to Caucasians; would that view, then, too, not be a form of influencing bias that could colour his work in the opposite direction? Couldn't a scientist, even one with more socially acceptable opinions, *still* be influenced by them in a way that skews their work?

Of course we needn't bother asking these questions. There are entire branches and divisions of discovery considered "touchy" by many members of the scientific community at large, including those revolving around differences of race, gender, and sexuality (because it would fuel bigoted supremacy groups), gene-editing (because it would involve questions as to when it is okay to change someone to fit a specific end, even beneficial), the ethics of robotics and when something should be treated as a person or as a tool (because of questions revolving around consciousness and what makes it special to be human), greater studies into nature vs nurture (because if it seems nature is victorious, you could theoretically categorize humans by D.N.A alone), and studies as to the role culture plays in one's psyche and what that would mean for society at large.

Sensitive topics also include more niche social categories that would otherwise cause civil unrest, such as studies into parenting, the regulation and long-term effects of generic drug and medication use, whether robots should replace workers, the damage and danger of advertisements and breaking news, the use of aborted fetuses to conduct medical research, the damage idealization does to one's psyche and its prevalence in media in the digital age, deep studies into religion and its practitioners, whether humans should be cloned at all, whether humans should be tested upon at all, whether or not organ donation should be mandatory, studies into factory farming, the 'utopian' society and who is required to make it, and the use of nanotechnology, among many others.

Even in attempting to write a research paper, you may be gently guided away from topics that could bring up controversy, or even more gently guided into findings that bring the most cash-benefit.

It seems even the crowd that traditionally shouts to the moon about the importance of following truth wherever it goes and how it always prevails and can never be hidden for long, still shy away from investigating it when it makes them a bit uncomfortable in their ideology to do so.

Though, to their credit, that's the same with most people who tout 'Truth' as an underlying foundation of their ideology; because the problem is that truth is impartial and cares nothing for feelings, cohesion, or stability, and this makes it no friends among those who rather appreciate these things. Unfortunately, it seems the people we often trust most to find these truths *are not* impartial and *do* have care and concern for the effects their discoveries will have on society at large, for better or worse.

Which, I mean, fair enough I suppose. I care about society too, and all things being equal, it is better to trust someone who is corruptible and knows what they're doing than someone who is corruptible and doesn't. But it is *still* important to make that distinction. It is *still* important to know that academia is corruptible, politicized, and bias, and that they are *always* able to bend the truth when it suits their ends.

This is why I made the point earlier that the greatest wage of the scientist is the trust placed in their position; and that despite this dependence upon their expertise, we must always be vigilant, lest their position be abused to disastrous effect. As it has been in the past...

Andrew Wakefield was at one point a respected doctor and gastroenterologist at UCL Medical School, and he went on to cause the autism-vaccine scare of 1998 (which is still the foundation for the current anti-vax movement today). He pushed his own variant of the vaccine at greater cost to the buyer as well as an autism testing kit of his own design; neither of which were functional because the autism-causing disease he claimed to discover was unable to be found by any of his peers. His cohorts, John O'Leary (professor at Trinity College) and Hugh Fudenberg (Immunologist and former Chairman at MUSC) both swore up and down as to Wakefield's testimony and that they actually did find this autism-causing disease from their samples.

Completely unrelated, O'Leary had an 11.1% stake in Wakefield's prospective company which would have been selling the testing kits, and Fudenberg was listed on the patent as co-creator of the 'superior' vaccines that Wakefield tried to pitch, both being worth potentially millions of dollars of sales, and we know that because that was their selling point to prospective investors. (If you're interested in the full depth of this particular tale, I'd recommend Harris Brewis' incredible documentary "Vaccines and Autism: A Measured Response" about how the whole scare was started and the sheer depths people will go to for money and fame).

John Money was at one point a respected professor of pediatrics and medical psychology at Johns Hopkins Gender Identity Clinic, and in his pursuit of studies regarding sexology, gender identity, and sexual orientation, went on to mistreat and abuse two young boys, one of which, due to a botched circumcision, was raised as a girl at Money's insistence to test his theory as to gender being a social construct. To facilitate this, he had the victim's testicles removed, had all trace of the boy's original sex expunged as he was treated as a girl, given hormone treatments, and given a new name. To familiarize the victim with the "female identity", he encouraged the two (preadolescent) boys to perform sex acts on eachother and would observe them undressing and performing 'genital inspections' (which he took at least one photograph of), as described in the victim's biography written by John Colapinto.

Though Money described the experiments as successful, the victim and his brother did not agree, with the victim never identifying as a woman and 'reassigning themselves male' upon learning the truth of their sex. Didn't end up helping though, both boys ending up killing themselves, citing both the trauma, abuse, and lack of support as main culprits in their suicide.

Patrick Moore was at one point a respected specialist in forest biology who's claim to fame was co-founding Greenpeace and bringing attention to the destructive testing of nuclear detonations by the American and French governments, as well as raising awareness and funding to protect whales from predatory fishing practices. Nowadays, after his split from Greenpeace, all he's famous for is consulting on behalf of corporations who rely upon fossil fuels and oil as main exports, and speaking in defense of companies like Monsanto who did not disclose the cancer-causing carcinogens in their weed killing products; all so that these same corporations can sound more environmentally friendly than they actually are. I presume.

Harry Harlow was at one point a respected doctor specializing in the psychology of animal behaviour at University of Wisconsin-Madison, who's work and research with Rhesus Monkeys and their attachment to surrogates paved the way to new findings of the importance of parental affection and guidance in a young child's life (which, up to this point, had largely been seen as a 'wasteful' and 'sentimental' effort). After the death of his second wife in her struggle with cancer, Harlow was said to have become a bitter, sadistic man, whose efforts shifted from the importance of love and maternal care to, seemingly, reveling in the joy of *depriving* animals of their mothers and playmates, leaving them in dark, cramped isolation chambers for up to a year in something he coined *"the pit of despair"*, strapping them to *"rape racks"* where he would entice vicious fornication from other members of the species whilst the victim could neither run nor fight back, and devising surrogates that tortured the Rhesus Monkey babies by spraying them with ice-cold water, hitting them across the room, or pricking them with sharp spikes. One of Harlow's former students, William Mason, wrote of the experience:

"[he] kept [the experiments] going to the point where it was clear to many people that the work was really violating ordinary sensibilities, that anybody with respect for life or people would find this offensive."

When inquired as to his treatment of the Rhesus Monkeys, Harlow responded,

"The only thing I care about is whether the monkeys will turn out a property I can publish."

For his efforts in studying a few monkeys and torturing many more, Harlow won a national medal of science based on his findings, in addition to being named the president of the American Psychological Association, which, as part of its duties, is meant to oversee ethical conduct in research, which for some unfathomable reason he was chosen as the most fit to do so. But hey, at least he didn't say there was a link between D.N.A and intelligence, so he's obviously overqualified.

Joseph Goldberger was at one point a highly respected (and still is, actually; he's just dead now) doctor and epidemiologist who specialized in epidemics and outbreak diseases. He had a long and gold-spun history of rigorous and selfless service as he fought (and caught) diseases such as yellow fever, typhoid, dengue fever, and typhus; and he was the one who figured out that Pellagra, a long-time enemy of the working-class American South, was an ailment born of a lack of nutrition rather than germs. He studied the diets common to orphanages and sanitariums (which was mostly corn based) and arranged that they be given a lean protein-heavy diet instead, not only finding that it prevented pellagra, but cured it.

He went even further, supplementing his findings with experiments where he induced pellagra in prisoners via a protein-deficient diet in exchange for their pardons. The academic community at the time dismissed this finding, however; stating that it must have been latent germs instead. So as a proper scientist, Goldberger threw a now infamous 'filth' party where he and select researchers (who volunteered, thankfully) tried to catch pellagra through varied germ-infested means, including blood injections from those suffering from pellagra, contaminated tissues stuffed up their own noses, contaminated throat swabs, and crafted a pill made from a mixture of the feces, urine, and scabs of the victims... which they then swallowed. Among all who attended, none caught pellagra through these methods.

Not that it mattered. This too was dismissed by critics and peers; for this experiment involved mostly men, and *of course* everyone knew that women were more susceptible to the disease. Goldberger has having a rough time, because he was not up against just the disease, but also 'The Thompson-McFadden Commission', a group of doctors and researchers who found that there was no link between pellagra and diet, and that germs were the most probable cause. By complete coincidence, the Thompson-McFadden Commission was funded heavily by Southern-dominant oil and cotton corporations (as reported in the National Library of Medicine) and to say that pellagra was caused by a nutrient-deficient diet was to say that Southern businesses didn't pay their workers a wage where they could afford healthy food, and how would they attract an influx of workers and business tourism then?

It wasn't until 1916, after two years of fighting the commission, that Goldberger's findings were taken seriously, and he successfully campaigned to have Brewer's Yeast (which he found cured Pellagra though he knew not why) distributed by the Red Cross amongst care rations to those suffering from displacement and poverty. Make no mistake, Joseph Goldberger is a hero who risked his life time and again to help cure the diseases that have been haunting mankind for thousands of years, but in remembering his story we must also remember the damage that the Semmelweis-reflex can have; as most doctors of Goldberger's era were smitten with the idea that everything could be explained with germs; as well as the ever-looming threat of lobbying in Academia to maintain preferred results over the truth.

Santiago Genovés was an anthropologist affiliated with the National Autonomous University of Mexico who experimented on the effects of isolation and close proximity by intentionally misleading ten volunteers into being trapped on a boat for 101 days in the 'Peace Project/Acali Experiment' where he verbally and psychologically abused them with the intent of promoting either extreme lust or violence, up to, and including, their own death. The crew remained friendly and peaceful even as Genovés allegedly repeatedly encouraged conflict; such as attempts to instill grudges by lying about what other passengers thought about another, mistreating one and favouring another, encouraging hazing, encouraging racist viewpoints, encouraging sexist viewpoints, and intentionally leaving knives and an axe out in the open to be used in any spontaneous rage. Luckily, by the end of the trip when the crew were forced to commandeer the boat and sail it away from the danger Genovés sailed them into, the only person they ended up with a plan to kill was Genovés himself in case he grew erratic and tried to sink the ship or something.

Bharat Aggarwal, formerly Professor of Cancer Research at the MD Anderson Cancer Center was struck from the board after it was found that he tampered with up to 65 of his research papers, showing a fraudulent link between specific chemical components and the curing of cancer, with the supposed motivation of promoting his own company selling alternative cures.

. . .

Werner Bezwoda, formerly of the University of Witwatersrand, was dismissed after scientific misconduct in trials on the positive effects of bone-marrow transplants on breast cancer where he altered results to be overwhelmingly positive. Motivated by, as far as anyone found, a distinct desire for fame.

Joachim Boldt, an anesthesiologist based at the University of Giessen, was stripped of his professorship over charges of fabricating data in his research studies. To this day, many papers authored or co-authored by Boldt remain in open-source publication to be read by prospective surgeons, causing a serious risk to all patients put under the care of his methods.

C. David Bridges, a professor of biology at Purdue University, was found by a NIH investigation panel to have plagiarized from a colleague's manuscript he was asked to review, and falsifying records in an attempt to claim the discovery for himself.

Chemist Annie Dookhan of Hinton Laboratory, Massachusetts, had charges pressed over altering test results and adulterating samples in order to cover up misconduct, as well as giving the green light on untested drug samples; actions which resulted in the potential contamination of tens of thousands of drug kits and the potential wrongful criminal conviction of drug possession for anyone unfortunate enough to be tested by one. It is worth noting that though she was only investigated in 2011, a probe by state police revealed that her superiors had been ignoring concerning behaviour and red flags for potentially years.

. . .

Diederik Stapel, former professor of social psychology at Tilburg University, and author/co-author of the works *"Coping with Chaos"*, *"Selfishness of Carnivores"*, *"The Effects of Prime Awareness on Social Judgements"*, and *"From (Unconscious) Perception to Emotion"*, among others, fabricated data in dozens of studies on behaviour found within said works. So if you read any of those, sorry about that. He even got a feature in the New York Times, titled "Audacious Academic Fraud," and has since had 58 of his publications retracted.

On the grander scale of horrific events, after a staggering rough 107 papers on tumor biology had to be retracted after editors found, quote: *"strong reason to believe that the peer review process was compromised,"* and an investigation was called into China's Ministry of Science and Technology over how this could be. This led to the discovery of a fraudulent peer-review ring where researchers would bolster eachother up in order to get the green light and receive more funding from the years 2012 to 2016. A rough 510 separate cancer researchers were charged, most of whom were found guilty with the rest being put under observation.

There is also the tragic story of Doris Stauffer who, at 74, succumbed to Alzheimer's disease which, by all medical accounts, she didn't carry the gene for. This was a startling revelation, because it means she *might* have mutated it, which would open up a whole new horizon into the disease and how it worked. Because of this, medical officials pleaded with her son, Jim Stauffer, to grant them rights over the body to perform research and find whether or not this was so, and Stauffer granted it. Her regular neurologist was not available, and so a nurse at the hospital recommended the Biological Resource Center (BRC) in Phoenix, headed by Stephen Gore. Stauffer signed the agreement that his mother's brain would be used exclusively for Alzheimer's research and handed over the body, whereupon, days later, he received a box from BRC containing her ashes with assurances that her brain would go on to save many lives.

Three years later, a journalist uncovering cases of medical fraud found documents detailing that Mr. Stauffer was *not*, in fact, sent the ashes of his mother's body, but only of her hand, with the rest of her body, including the brain, being sold off, for profit, to a military complex to use in blast testing. The brain doctors begged to perform research on was never once touched by a scalpel. BRC and military records show that at least 20 other bodies were also used in the blast experiments without permission of the donors or their relatives, and even the military itself seemed to have no knowledge of where these bodies were being sourced: relying upon falsified documents from the BRC itself. When BRC facilities were raided by the FBI, they allegedly found a Frankenstein-esque horror show, with potentially hundreds of bodies being placed haphazardly, hacked apart, and auctioned as requested, with almost none having proper identification or paperwork to go with their requested treatment. BRC, it seemed, was running a body-snatching ring where they would request bodies of the recently deceased for research only to turn and falsify documents in order to sell them to industrial complexes and organ harvesters for profit and was doing so for over a decade with thousands of bodies being misplaced in the process, as reported by Reuters.

It is worth noting that Stephen Gore, the director of this body-snatching ring, not only had zero credentials as to actually authorize the taking and storing of these bodies for their *stated* use, but never even went to college. He was able to deceive people, not out of true academic knowledge, but through the appearance of academia alone. The trust so imbued.

And, of course, 'The Sugar Conspiracy', in which, during the formulative years of nutrition science in 1943, select food companies formed a board referred to as the: Sugar Research Foundation (SRF), with the stated goal of: *"Dedication to the scientific study of sugar's role in food."* The SRF managed this by sponsoring and funding Harvard researchers who published articles that downplayed the link between sugar and heart disease, and overinflated research that found fat as the culprit. The reviews were published in the New England Journal of Medicine in 1967, with no disclosure of backing by the SRF. Cristin Kearns, Laura Schmidt, and Stanton Glantz (the three who have gone on to review the SRF's conclusions in their article for JAMA Internal Medicine) find no evidence that any research was 'directly' tampered with, but they *did* discover documents promising the Harvard researchers that payments of what amounts to $50,000 U.S dollars would be provided for each "successful" article showing a greater link between fat and heart disease or for efforts to discredit articles that linked it with sugar instead. Promises which were never disclosed to the board, as reported by STAT News.

Marion Nestle, a nutrition expert at New York University is even more pessimistic with her own findings in JAMA Internal Medicine:

"In 2015, the New York Times obtained emails revealing Coca-Cola's cozy relationships with sponsored researchers who were conducting studies aimed at minimizing the effects of sugary drinks on obesity. Even more recently, the Associated Press obtained emails showing how a candy trade association funded and influenced studies to show that children who eat sweets have healthier body weights than those who do not."

This was a battle also fought by John Yudkin (physiologist and nutritionist, as well as founding Professor of the Department of Nutrition at Queen Elizabeth College) which culminated in his flagship work, "Pure, White, and Deadly" in 1972, a summarization of all research correlating sugars, fructose, and glucose with obesity and heart disease. It was a battle he regrettably seemed to lose, as a mix of lobbying, strong-arming, and pure dismissal from his fellows prevented the work from being taken seriously; only being accepted in the early 2000's, and only gaining true traction in the 2010's.

. . .

Despite what this list might imply, note that I am only bringing them up as an example to my point that academia is corruptible. In reality, most cases of misconduct within the scientific community affect *only* the scientific community. Plagiarism or theft of work are among the most common offenses, with Daniele Fanelli's article *"How Many Scientists Fabricate and Falsify Research?"* finding only 2% of scientists falsifying, fabricating, or modifying data and 33% engaging in 'questionable' research practices (though it is worth noting that these are just those who *admitted* to doing so). It is funny then, that where experts are concerned, reminding people that human beings have the capacity to lie and be susceptible to internal bias is the act of a radical.

This is only corruption that has been *proven*, by the way. It is to say nothing of suspicious behaviours, seemingly clashing interests, or prospective underhanded dealings; like Katherine Ellen Foley's fabulous reporting in her QUARTZ article "Trust Issues Deepen", where she points out that nine out of the last ten FDA commissioners (for the last 38 years at the time the article was written) have gone on to work in the pharmaceutical industry as board members, directors, and presidents. Very cushy positions indeed.

Or Ben Goldacre, Fellow at the Institute of Psychiatry in London (among his many other awards) who has seemingly made it his life's mission to call out bad science, whether it be quackery, pseudo-science, or more alarming issues like what he notes in his TedTalk: *"What Doctors Don't Know About The Drugs They Prescribe"*, how a rough half of all drug trials are not made publicly available (so that risky and dangerous practices take longer to be found), and positive findings are twice as likely to be published as negative ones, giving undue incentive.

. . .

Or Charles Piller and Jia You's article: *"Hidden conflicts?"* where they detail investigations showing how, among other things, FDA advisors were paid anywhere from tens of thousands and in some cases up to a million dollars by select pharmaceutical companies after giving their prospective drug a green-light. A clear conflict of interest that by-and-large goes unreported and unconsidered.

Or how, since the 1970's, a rough 50% of publishing in science has been under the domain of just five companies. *'SAGE'*, *'Taylor and Francis'*, *'Springer'*, *'Elsevier'*, and *'Wiley-Blackwell'*, with most of them not having the most respectable history as far as Pure-Academia is concerned.

Or Victor M. Toledo's report on the corruption of science on an **international** level, along with the 'Union of Concerned Scientists' (UCS) report, *"Heads They Win, Tails We Lose"* which details the methods of abuse and coercion that many corporations use to get results they desire from research reports.

I reiterate, above all else, that I am not trying to promote an anti-scientific method form of thinking, nor am I trying to demonize academics or portray them as power hungry or foolish. I am only trying to prove that some of them *are*; that much like with some general practitioners who do not even test for your ailments and just insist you're faking it, or with some teachers who ignore the problems of bullying, or with some fire stations who have an unfortunate history of employing hero-complex arsonists who set the fire themselves in order to have the glory of putting it out, that perhaps we should recognize that virtue is a quality of character and not profession.

. . .

So you can see why it makes me a little nervous when I see opinion pieces that suggest academics should use their positions of trust and expertise to urge for certain social, political, or economic policies; especially because we have historical precedence for why that is a bad idea when, circa 1940, tobacco companies used doctors and their image to push the legitimacy of their claims between smoking and health. Despite this, and despite all the harm it can do, many lobbyists still try to push these views through academia anyways, as if any word that came from a scientist were a divine gospel to which it was heresy to question; a view I'm sure you realize many corrupt corporations and researchers can take advantage of today.

In such an environment where the opinion of one person, bolstered by the media, can radically shift society and beliefs for years to come; and in an industry where even those with the best intentions can err, where medical malpractice and error alone contributes to the third leading cause of death in America as reported by Johns Hopkins; it is not only unethical, but *harmful* to suggest that academics are above scrutiny. If Detective Novels have taught me anything, it's that the person you should be most suspicious of is the last person to see the victim alive; not because they're the most likely suspect, but because they are the only faucet from which information about the circumstances flows without being able to be contradicted or critically examined by another.

Nobody, neither mortal or divine, individual or group, is ever above scrutiny, and those trying to convince you that they are do *not* have your best interests at heart.

Some people will look at all this and argue that separate facilities and universities could become corrupt, sure, and that's why it's best to look at universal consensus, to which I would remind them that, if the truth were closer to consensus, it would mean babies couldn't feel pain up until the late 1980's and Thalidomide was fine for pregnant women. Because, hey, I hate to break it to you, but all of the above scrutiny's were just times where researchers were *trying* to hide what they were doing wrong. We haven't even gotten to issues plaguing modern science by sheer dint of accident and circumstance, through no fault of the faculty's own.

Vox's article, *"The Seven Biggest Problems Facing Science"* covers a paltry handful, like how most money in academia is gained through the publishing of research papers which cause a feedback loop of quantity over quality; or the publishing houses themselves and how they incentivize 'bigger, bolder' discoveries over smaller, meaningful ones, pushing academics to alter their works, even down to the language used, so that discoveries *seem* more groundbreaking and impressive than they actually are; or the lack of replication due to stronger incentives to focus on finding *new* information over checking old kinds, bungled peer review (due to numerous issues, including a lack of reward for actually checking your peers' work, a lack of specialists who can review your work reliably, and researchers prioritizing their own investigations before reviewing others), or scientists being either legally or financially obliged to put their work behind paywalls, causing other researchers and reviews to have to pay out of pocket to have the supplemental material, which in turn incentivizes them to charge for their own research to recoup the costs; or the clickbait nature that publishers will use *to describe* discoveries, using the most positive wording (such as "cure for cancer") or negative wording (such as "die to death") in order to generate a higher viewer count and completely misrepresent the research; and, honestly, just the crummy lives of many of these researchers in general, who are treated as if they are contractors, given grueling hours, and paid little for their services relative to how much they *ought* to be paid for their level of education.

For yes, scientists *are* people; I believe I may have said that before, who knows, and yes I have been pointing out flaws in the field of academia for the whole of this essay, but these flaws stem from their *humanity*, for all the good and the bad that it entails, they are *people*, and they are just as deserving of sympathy and support as you or I, and perhaps if they got a little bit more of it they wouldn't be suffering from depression and suicide to the point of climbing the list on every chart crossing profession with poor mental health.

I've heard "real science" being described as having the willingness to change with new evidence, a ruthless peer review, inviting criticism, repeatable results, and taking into account all new discoveries; but of course, as we've just learned, this isn't true. There is rarely a willingness to change even *with* new evidence; the lack of proper peer review is one of the greatest insider threats in academia, many celebrity scientists are *antagonistic* to their critics, and most experiments are so specialized that only a fraction of results are repeatable.

The idea of this 'true' science; this venerable, idealistic image of a perfect being, Doctor Dutchname McScientist, who is absolute in his reasonings, character, and information, from which all new discoveries descend, is little more than a fairy tale.

Throughout all of this, everything we just discussed, the one biggest takeaway should be what I've been trying to instill this entire time: That scientists are just people. For all the good and the bad. For all the hope and despair. For all the bias and virtue. For all the benevolence in trying to do the right thing and the selfishness of corruption.

They have been, and always will be, just people; populated by you, and I, and your neighbour, and that one office worker you really don't like, and that boss who chose his nephew over you when you totally deserved that promotion more, and that cute busybody at the grocery store who always smiles when they rack your things.

They are just people. So the next time some big discovery is made, ask them if they're really super extra sure about the findings of their studies and then cut them some slack if they tell you they don't know.

And if you happen to be an Academic and have gotten through this entire essay instead of passing it off as the ramblings of some anti-science nutcase, fantastic, I applaud you, you are my favourite kind of person, and this conclusion is for you.

If you, or any of your peers, are aware of strange going's-on's or are worried that someone has been altering their research or even if you just feel nervous that what you might be doing may not be the most ethical, never ever be afraid to speak up. Even going outside of your field and contacting a journalist, most of whom would be happy to perform their own independent investigation and leave you completely out of it. If you are suffering from depression and anxiety, talk to someone. Talk to your friends. Talk to your loved ones. Talk to those who will understand you and accept your worries with all the grace and dignity they deserve. If you are concerned with the state of academia and where your profession may be going and the opportunities available to you, seek out circles with similar concerns, contact unions, there are hundreds of people who would love to hear from you to be able to help you where you need it most.

Being caught in these kinds of things can suck, but taking proactive steps to try to correct it and ferret out the truth and make sure all is as it should be is worth it. And together, between holding academia responsible for its screw ups and raising awareness for the struggles and problems within, we can both, all of us, one by one, mend the problems that prevent us from moving forward to where we should be.

And isn't that the job of a scientist too?

ON LOVE AND ROMANCE

"*We accept the love we think we deserve.*"
 - Stephen Chbosky

*M*any people go throughout their lives searching for that 'special someone', that one person they can share everything with; whether about themselves, their past, their present, or their future, and yet in all of this the question of *how* to cultivate love rarely comes up.

Do yourself a favour and think about the qualities you find attractive. What you desire in a partner. Have you been in love before? What qualities did they possess? Really introspect. Go ahead. I'll be here when you get back.

Excellent, now think on *why* you love these qualities. Why are they important to you? Why do you want them in a partner? Now hold that thought for a minute.

As cliché as it may sound, the best thing someone can do when looking for love is to be themselves.

Don't misunderstand, I'm not saying that you're the specialist pea in the pod, I'm not your mother. What I'm saying is that it is easier to cultivate a love born from being who you are than pretending to be someone you are not. That goes for trying to be like that super cool character from your favourite media to even just lying to your prospective partner. Try not to do that. For if you are not yourself when searching for love then those who return it will not be in love with *you*, but whom they perceive you to be.

If, on the other hand, you are one of those unfortunate folks with low self-esteem and can't find anything in yourself worth loving... then why are you looking?

The first and most skipped step in searching for true love is that you must first learn to love YOURSELF. Ultimately, if you cannot love yourself, how could anyone else? If you cannot respect yourself, why do you think others could find a reason to? If you honestly see nothing in yourself worth loving then it is not "looking for love" that is your problem, but finding it within yourself. And even more damaging; if you do not love yourself, how could you love *them* properly? Could you really love *them*? Or would you only love the way they loved *you*? Not who they were, but how they made you feel.

That is the risk. Because those who are without love believe that in having it, all their wants will be fulfilled. All their self-doubt, their self-hatred, their denial, their shame, everything they dislike would be burned away by the power of this love. And yet it is not so. That is why there are so many people in terrible relationships, that is why there are so many who give so much to people who don't seem to give a damn, because it is not out of love for this person; but the validation *received* from them, the big bright stamp that declares 'You Are Worth Loving'. But it cannot last.

There is no amount of love that would ever make up for not loving yourself; and eventually the honey-moon phase will end, and you will desire more, and demand more, and when they cannot love you in the way you wish, the way you want to love yourself, you will find it is not enough. It could never be enough. Just as there is no amount of love that can cure mental illness, so too is there no amount of love that can make up for our own disharmony. It is something we must resolve for ourselves, *within* ourselves; and while love can *support* us, it cannot make up for what we lack.

It is difficult to love yourself. As it can be to love anyone when we know all of the ways in which they fail, all of the ways in which they feel frightened, or inadequate; all of the ways which we feel uncomfortable with or despise or feel guilt over. But it can still be done. *Must* be done. Because most people do not know what love is.

Remember when I asked you to hold that thought before? Great, I'm so glad, because here's where you put it. When thinking of the qualities of the person you would fall for, were they actually *real?* Were they *human* qualities? Or just some nebulous traits that are associated with 'goodness'? Beauty. Ambition. Intelligence. These things tell you nothing about who someone *is*, they are only qualities we find respectable. Qualities we want to be worthy of.

When people think of themselves; not asked to describe themselves, but just think of themselves, on their own term, they often do not imagine these kinds of traits; but are more down-to-earth. They think of themselves in the way they grumble and groan, or the way they look when they smile, or the jokes they laugh too hard at; often poorly, often feeling self-conscious, but it is these qualities that make up romantic life far more than any other. It can sound strange encouraging people to find love in the way someone gets out of bed, or the way they sip their coffee, or they way they sigh when they plop onto the couch, and yet *these* are the intimate moments. The way you love them when they think you're not looking. And the same is said for you too.

It is one thing to puff your chest and be proud of how much money you make; it is entirely another to be proud of the way you still take your dogs for a walk even when you're dead-tired. To be proud of the restraint you show in not buying those cookies because you *really* gotta get working on those new-year resolutions and you know you failed the last five times but you really wanna do it this time and you're really really gonna because *these* are the same moments you will share with the one you love.

I urge you toward self-love because trying to rush into a relationship out of loneliness or lust will invariably lead to far more pain than it ever could joy; and it will do so from both sides. We have a responsibility to ourselves, in our wisdom, to make what we know are the right choices.

Now that you've had five seconds to chew on that, I'll give you some actual advice. Love is a two-way street. As said from the beginning, nearly everyone is looking for love and for someone to share their life with, but you cannot find someone to share your life with if you stay cooped up into yourself all day. You must put yourself OUT there, show your colours as a peacock does to its mate, and give your desired prospects a reason to consider you an option. This doesn't always mean going to parties or being super-extroverted, but you do have to actually talk to people. And remember what I said near the start about you having to be honest with them about who you are and not put up a mask. You have to actually be *known*. Horrifying, I know. But it's a requirement. You could be the most interesting person on Earth and nobody would ever know it if you were too shy to share it.

And **please** spruce yourself up. Seriously. Shave. Shower. Use cologne and perfume. *"Hurr durr but you said I should be who I am,"* you sputter, spewing grease everywhere, reaching into the bag for yet another corn-chip before I smack it out of your hands and remind you that the goal is to be YOURSELF and for yourself to be BETTER. Go on more walks. Consult someone with actual fashion sense. Eat a fucking banana. You're not cursed to live as a piglet until some sweet soul loves you for who you are like the Beast in its tower; it shouldn't be some kind of *test* for them to win your cheese-dusted hand.

Now that you've gone through that little montage and returned after making yourself more attractive, now comes the part where you go to those you want to *attract*. You wouldn't go out to a pub to talk about politics or ancient literature; neither would you talk about what makes a fine meal while in a medical center. You must go to places where your hobbies and preferences are praised and can be refined by the opinions and criticism of others, so not only are you able to grow as a person, but also just have a higher chance of meeting the type of person you want to court. Just make sure *they* know you're interested. It's not creepy to say someone is sweet enough to go on a date with once you've actually gotten to know them; and if they *are* interested in you and you wait too long to make it known (or they're just a silly goose who has trouble picking up hints) they might get the impression you're not interested.

That's really all there is to it, become what you admire, love yourself, find a place where you can find those *you* admire, and then just make friends. And never be afraid to take the first step either. A shocking number of problems in life could be avoided simply by acting sooner rather than later, and romance is no different. Of course, then, there is everything else that comes after.

Relationships are based on communication. Most people know this, and most will tell you to listen, but what most don't mention is that you also need to talk. Remember that bit about being who you are and not trying to hide everything behind a mask? Yeah, that goes for your feelings and concerns too. Hiding yourself away from someone you want an attachment with is like thinning a string with the hope it gets stronger. You must learn to accept yourself and your partner, both their success and their failures, if you want to form a relationship and they must do the same for you. If either party is unable to do so, then perhaps kindling a romance with them should not be your top priority.

There was a wonderful little internet post I saw a long time ago where someone talks about how they took a course in relationships and the lecturer told them that people often fall out of love for the same reasons they fell *in* love. It is only that, through time, what qualities were once endearing becoming agitating. Spending money freely is no longer seen as spontaneous and fun-loving, but reckless and irresponsible; disorganization is no longer seen as a detachment from the little things and instead becomes a disregard for one's living space; passion is no longer seen as energetic and romantic but becomes temperamental and overly emotional; and the reason it all shifts from one thing to another is because our goals change. Our circumstances change. Our life changes. You must think outward, beyond this moment; who will this person be ten years from now? Who will *you* be? Will you be suited for eachother then? These are harrowing questions. I understand if you do not want to think of them today. But if you don't think of them at some point, you may find yourself with someone you barely recognize without ever knowing why.

Next, do not be afraid to challenge them, and face challenges with them. Not to say you ought to intentionally push their buttons, but only to remember that relationships are a partnership too. If you begin treating them like some sort of love dispensary wherein you input love and get love back, it just circles around to the first issue all over again. It is okay to discuss deeper subjects, it is okay to disagree, it is okay to treat them like a friend.

Third, if it does not work out, be it friendship, relationship, whatever, don't be afraid to end it. This is something many people have trouble with because they delude themselves into thinking that love can spark up again; but love does not spark, it GROWS, just like the Earth and foliage around you. If you stay in a relationship longer, hoping that after a certain amount of time (or worse, children) you will fall back in love, you are only delaying the inevitable. You must never sacrifice self-love for anything; if you must stop loving yourself, or lose what you love about yourself in order to be loved by someone else, then it is not you that they love and it is simply not worth it. Do not be deluded by feelings of comfort and coziness. That being 'used' to this person is worth a lack of love. It is not; for it is as the first line of this essay goes: We accept the love we think we deserve, and the more we accept poorer treatment and the more we accept apathy, the more we feel we deserve it. Do not allow yourself to be whittled away; because it will not make your life easier, it will only cause you to think back and ask yourself what happened.

For many, the only quest is to feel loved; and they are willing to pursue whatever means necessary to get it. A shame. "Those without love think it will solve all their problems" and those with self-love know that it is the most fulfilling, validating love of all.

THE BAKUGO REFLEX

One half a dissertation on character-writing, and the other an exploration of social phenomena.
I wrote this for me, not for you.

S o some time ago I watched an anime; abbreviated as MHA, it is called 'My Hero Academia' or 'Boku No Hero Academia' if you're a total dweeb.

It is... adequate, as far as Shonen anime goes. The premise is that in this world, some high percentage of people are born with some type of superpower. Though this power can be genetically influenced via ancestry, the degree and style in which it manifests appears random. Some are more pragmatic than others. Due to this, there are some who have styled themselves as superheroes, and have created a school in which people with these more pragmatic types of powers can go and hone their abilities before becoming heroes themselves. There is a hero ranking that shows how popular each hero is, and there is a bit of a sub-plot and cultural conflict regarding heroes as they attempt to reach the top. Simple.

It is very tropey while also taking a stab at deconstructing these tropes, and while it doesn't always make the most sense, I appreciated it for what it was. Mostly. Except for one part.

For you see, there is this character in the show. His name is Bakugo.

Bakugo takes the role of the rival to the (at this point powerless) main protagonist Deku. Bakugo's power is not only extremely offensive, by way of causing controlled explosions, but it is also exceedingly powerful. He is well aware of this and uses his status as a shoo-in for this hero academy to domineer those around him as he pursues his quest to become the greatest hero alive. He is arrogant, brash, and downright villainous; his introductory scene opens with declaring how much better he is than everyone else, *especially* the main character, before going over and *destroying their most prized possession*, and maliciously encouraging him to *kill himself* so that he may have the chance to be reincarnated into someone with a superpower.

Now, if you've had any experience with bullies, this scene might have raised your cortisol levels, and even if you *didn't*, it may have risen some red flags. This behaviour seems wildly excessive for the point it is trying to make. More than just a character establishing themselves as a 'rival', this is what you'd expect from a *bad person*.

Which is completely fine. I've enjoyed my fair share of media and find both antagonists and anti-heroes to possess their own charm. I'm fine with a character being a bad person.

The problem is that the series doesn't seem to *realize* that he is.

If you haven't seen the series, you're just going to have to trust me: Bakugo is regularly flippant with his superiors, demeaning and domineering to his peers, he regularly threatens people with bodily harm if they go against his will or so much as disagree with him, he has repeatedly stated that he would rather die than be a team-player, and on one occasion, bucked direct orders from a superior in favour of putting a fellow student at risk of extreme harm. (The context is: during a training session, he sought out his rival, proceeded to begin using his 'ultimate power', was ordered by the teacher overseeing to stand down and told that a direct blast from such an attack could kill someone, to which Bakugo responds: *"He'll be fine as long as he dodges!"* and uses it anyways).

Now, in case you're not familiar with legal code, in any sane society that last little diddy there would get you immediately expelled, blacklisted from the facility you were training in, blacklisted from any facility you *could* train in, put on a psyche-evaluation, and then if not thrown into an asylum, promptly charged with attempted murder. I know that may be very hard to believe, but it actually *is* frowned upon to put someone's life at risk over your superiority complex.

Of course this is a fictional setting, and these are fictional characters, so some liberties are bound to be taken; I would just expect those liberties to be anything aside from what actually happens: Nothing.

He is never punished for any of this. He is never even chastised.

On the contrary, the anime itself seems to go out of its way to portray these actions in a comedic light. The protagonist will never miss a chance to encourage or support this person who tormented him all their life, characters will hand-wave these ~~psychotic outbursts~~ temper tantrums as being funny at best and mildly annoying at worst, and teachers who previously expelled students for showing 'no potential' will instead just tiredly sigh at these same behaviours that are highly correlated with the probability of being a serial killer. For some reason, nearly every character in the show seems to view this individual in either a positive or a tolerable light; to the point where the hand of the creator is seen, so unreasonable is this favoritism bestowed and problematic incidents glossed over.

And when Bakugo's backstory is revealed, it gets even stranger.

There was no tragedy. There was no inciting incident. He simply got his powers, developed a superiority complex because of them, and one day when he fell into a stream, the protagonist offered to help him up and instead of seeing this act as normal behaviour for regular people in a functioning, polite society, Bakugo got so monumentally furious, perceiving it as him being looked down upon and 'needing' assistance, that he seemingly devoted the rest of his life to making everyone else feel as inferior as he felt in that moment. He wants to be the best hero, the most popular hero, the most beloved hero, to prove how superior he is to everyone else. That's it.

I fucking wish I was joking.

That's the reason he wanted this poor kid to kill himself. That's the reason he threatens to hurt people who don't obey his commands. That's the reason he attempted to kill a fellow student.

I do not know what high power allowed such a character depiction get past proof-reading, but I can only assume it was drugs.

"Cue, you're ranting again," you're damn right I am. Do you *know* how long this has been on my mind? I've lost SLEEP over getting my thoughts organized as to why this frustrates me so much, and what do you care!? YOU ALREADY READ THIS FAR! THIS IS MY ESSAY! *I WILL WRITE HOW I PLEASE AND YOU ARE GOING TO LIKE IT.*

Now, I honestly believed that this kind of writing would put a bit of a black streak on the show, but here's the kicker, and the thing that got me into writing this to begin with: Most of the fanbase doesn't seem to agree. Bakugo, despite all his terrible traits, regularly breaks into the leaderboards as a most-popular character to the delight of the fans. Most of them see no issue with his behaviour, nor with how it is handled, nor with how it is written; they *love* this guy, to the point where there is a common issue of people just making up reasons as to why he behaves this way; reasons unsupported by the canon of the show.

And this confuses me... because they don't do it with anyone else. There are other problematic characters, one of which is this strange grape-haired imp of a fellow whose sole existence seems to be predicated on being a pervert; and the show treats him accordingly, using him as the butt of all corresponding jokes and the characters treating him like a creep. The fans seem to agree with this estimation. They agree he should have been expelled from the school by now. You don't find anybody making up reasons as to why he might behave this way...

It's here, this disparity, that piqued my interest, and in my quest for omniscience I began asking fans of the show why they were willing to overlook these actions. Why allow the antics of one character to slide and not another? And the response I got was borderline unanimous:

> *"Well, none of the OTHER characters seem to mind."*

This, somehow, was always what it circled around to. Other people did not treat it like it was such a big deal, so they didn't either. Since, if it was *really* that bad, someone would have raised a fuss, right? And since they haven't, it must not be... Hm...

Now, storytelling goes back a long way. I would be disingenuous if I pretended there WEREN'T other, villainous characters that were still showered with arguably undeserved favour and limelight. There's even a trope referring to it: 'Easily Forgiven,' wherein, as declared, the bad guy is forgiven rather too easily for the audience's liking; and there are certain shows that have made rather a business out of forgiving tyrannical, abusive dictators to the point where it becomes tiresome even to the target audience; and some of these characters can be directly compared. MHA *was* originally based on the idea of dissecting these tropes and Bakugo *does* have his inspirations.

There is Vegeta, Saiyan Prince, rival to Goku, from the series Dragon Ball Z. He is extremely powerful, arrogant, brash, and oftentimes downright villainous. In his first appearance he makes no compunction at all about murdering innocent people in his quest to conquer the Earth and even kills his own allies should they fail him.

But of course, Vegeta *was* originally a villain before he became an anti-hero figure. He *was* actively evil and, more importantly, the heroic cast *treated him accordingly*; working together to beat his ass (repeatedly) until he calmed down. It is also worth noting that Vegeta was reared in a warrior culture where might made right. Power and strength were all that mattered and your ability to get away with murder was contingent entirely upon whether or not you were powerful enough to kill them in the first place.

This view is reinforced through lived experience, when an evil alien overlord wiped most of his species from the face of the galaxy, once more affirming that power was all that mattered. Vegeta was not only most of all that was left of his people, to carry on their spirit, but his father was the *king*. He was *born superior*. His latter arcs of plummeting back into villainy over playing second-fiddle to what amounted to a nobody is reflected in this lineage, his view of what a warrior ought to be, and what *he* ought to represent.

In contrast, Bakugo is just some fucking guy in the middle of modern-day Japan. He has no patronage to represent, no legacy to be concerned over, and no culture he was indoctrinated into.

Another frequent comparison is made between Bakugo and Sasuke Uchiha. Sasuke, rival to Naruto from the series... um... 'Naruto', is extremely powerful, arrogant, callous, and is oftentimes prone to villainous tendencies. While rarely outwardly cruel, his first appearances characterize him as ambitious, prideful, and unconcerned with anyone but himself; having a similar view as to the nature of might making right and having his own cultural backing to facilitate it; being descended from a particularly powerful clan that has historically been at the center of many conflicts.

It is later revealed that part of his stone-façade and obsession with power is due to a traumatic event; where the person he loved and trusted more than anyone went on to kill most of his family and friends. Sasuke's entire life goal is to become strong enough to take revenge on this person, while simultaneously protecting those he cares about even as he stays distant enough to never be hurt again. Most of his character arc is centered around the conflict between his conflicting obsession and the acceptance and love he receives from the friends he has made since, and it is *treated accordingly.*

In contrast, Bakugo lives a (relatively) normal life in a (relatively) normal setting. His family and friends are alive, well, and supportive, and his obsessions are of his own choosing.

There is no in-universe reason why the characters should be so forgiving toward him, going so far as to refer to him as their friend. Yet they do, and the audience reacts accordingly...

Do you see the tether here? This connection between how a character *acts*, and how others *react*? The idea that people are judging this character, not based on their own moral integrity, but on the tolerance others have for it.

And that's what makes *this show* in particular so special, because I've never before seen such a perfect example of this sort of reflex in the same media.

Because, you see... I told a little bit of a fib earlier.

There is *another* problematic character in this show that we can compare directly.

And he is called Endeavour.

. . .

Endeavour takes the role of rival to the (at this point vastly weak) top hero All-Might. Endeavour's power is not only extremely offensive, by way of causing infernos, but it is also exceedingly powerful. He is well aware of this and uses his status and wealth as one of the top heroes to dominate those around him as he pursues his quest to become the greatest hero alive. He is arrogant, he is brash, he is downright villainous; his introductory scene opens with an intimidating glare and angle as another character explains the abuse they have suffered at this person's hands.

For you see, Endeavour is only the *second* greatest hero; and this fact eats at him like nothing else.

He *obsesses* over it. He struggled for years to reach the top and when it became clear he was past his prime, he used his status to ensnare himself a wife with complementary abilities. He began getting her pregnant, raising the child to where they would develop powers, and if they did not develop in a satisfactory way, he would proceed to neglect them, as if they never existed, before focusing on the next child. When one was finally born with strong powers he approved of, he began a grueling training process that bordered on torture; because in his mind, if his son could become the top hero, it means he himself would have 'won'. This torture and abuse over his family continues to the point where the mother has a mental breakdown, scarring her son's face, and being sent off to a psychiatric facility. Not for her own well-being, but to prevent her from potentially ruining Endeavour's grand plan. The process continues. There are more beatings. More insults. More berating. More threats. More destruction.

Now, if you've had any experience with abusers, this scene might have made you uncomfortable, and even if you *didn't*, it may have risen some red flags. This behaviour seems wildly malicious for someone's personal obsession. More than just a character establishing themselves as a 'rival', this is what you'd expect from a *bad person*.

Which is completely fine. Because he *is* a bad person. The anime realizes that just fine.

Every character who is familiar with what he has been up to treats him with scorn and disdain. When the extent of his abuse is finally revealed, he is heavily demonized by the community at large. His son, his most prized masterpiece, regularly rebels against him and more or less treats him like the scum of the earth at any given opportunity.

The anime explains his backstory; he saw his father die and wanted to prevent things like that from happening again, so he wants to be the best. Easy peasy. It doesn't really fit with anything we've seen up to now because how would that ambition have anything to do with pushing your *son* into being the top hero as a replacement, and why would you get upset wi- you know what, I'm getting off track. The point is, he developed a superiority complex and was angry he wasn't the best. He wants to be the best hero, the most popular hero, the most beloved hero, to prove how superior he is to everyone else. That's it.

That's the reason he neglected his family. That's the reason he threatens to hurt people who don't obey his commands. That's the reason he abused his children.

And the fans *hate* this son of a bitch. For the longest time, all anyone discussed about this character was how much of a dick he was; and even now that he started on his redemption arc (because of course), many people STILL have trouble accepting it, thinking he got off easy... and the *characters treat him accordingly.*

You may have noticed some shared traits between these descriptions of Bakugo and Endeavour.

These characters are not dissimilar. In fact, I'd go so far as to say that these similarities were *intentional* if not for the fact that they're never called into attention in any significant way, and Todoroki, the child whose life was made hell by his abusive father, considers Bakugo, a person who is almost exactly *like* his father, a good friend, for some unfathomable reason. I have trouble imagining nobody told the author that people don't tend to make friends with those who resemble their abusers.

Because they really *are* alike. Both characters have the ambition to be the best, they both have superiority complexes, they both have attitude problems, they both have sociopathic tendencies, they are both anti-social, they both consider others as tools to be used as a means to an end, their pride and anger are their main weaknesses, they both have a weird one-sided rivalry thing going on, and even their powers are of a similar destructive make-up.

And so we can see, point blank, the main difference between the two. Why people love one, and loath the other. It is in how the people around them *treat* them. One's threat of violence is viewed as a funny quirk, and the other is viewed as a heinous threat, and they are viewed this way from *within the narrative of the show.*

"Because none of the other characters seem to mind."

I talk a lot, as you can probably infer. I really like to make my opinions known about a great number of issues and I'm rather harsh on a lot of different places and peoples for what I consider to be backwards policies. When I express this, I am often met with a lukewarm defense:

"It is not our place to criticize it, it is just part of their culture"

and I'd believe this far more if these same people who said so didn't turn around and criticize other cultures closer to home for similar, oppressive issues. When I try to point this out, I get a similar response:

"But we know it's wrong!"

to which, of course they mean the people around them do. As if moral rights and wrongs changed from place to place, and from where people found certain things acceptable or not.

The sense of confusion at seeing a screaming child being slapped with a sandal by an angry parent and *not* seeing anyone jump in to stop it. That maybe it's just how things are done. Or being criticized because you gave money to the homeless and so begin to wonder if it's the wrong thing to do.

Or a more domestic example:

Have you ever been to someone's house, and saw family dynamics or odd behaviour that you were uncertain about, and yet accepted it because if it's something *they're* okay with, then you should be okay with it too?

Or times where you were with a group and did something you were raised to believe was bad, but nobody accosted you over it, causing you to wonder if it was really that bad after-all?

This is an example of what I have now coined: 'The Bakugo Reflex.'

Different from snap moral judgements based off of extenuating circumstance, incomplete information, or personal flaw; the Bakugo Reflex is when a moral judgement is made or second-guessed based on the reactions of those *around* the dilemma.

Likewise, this reconsideration of moral action cannot be based off of a desire for favoritism and approval from the in-group. If you know what is right and wrong, but do not act accordingly because you do not want to rock the boat, that isn't the Bakugo Reflex, but simply succumbing to peer-pressure. Instead, the reaction (or lack thereof) from those present must cause you to actually recontextualize how 'good' or 'bad' a certain thing *is*.

If you were in a dilemma where the right thing to do seemed obvious, but those around you reacted poorly to you considering it, causing you to question whether or not it was a good thing to do, *that* would be an example of the Bakugo Reflex. Just as well, if you were witness to something that was clearly morally wrong, but nobody else seemed to consider it so, and this caused you to doubt your faith in your own moral principles, that would be another example of the Bakugo Reflex.

Just to be clear, this reflex is not a constant, it does not affect everyone at all times, and there are those (such as from sheltered homes) who would be more liable to have it than others. Likewise, it isn't always a bad thing. There are times where it is *good* that the reactions of others cause us to self-examine. I'm just writing about it now because I could not get it out of my head for the past year and the dog started looking at me funny when I began talking to myself.

I hate Bakugo so god damn much it's unreal.

MUSINGS

LITTLE THOUGHTS THAT CANNOT BE EXTRAPOLATED INTO AN ESSAY YET ARE WORTH PONDERING REGARDLESS

*G*rand ideas can remain good ones; the broad strokes from the foundation of the painting; but as circumstances and societies change, so too should the minutiae of how we interact with ideas. Marcus Aurelius was one of the greatest rulers to ever live, and his meditations are still of value even today, thousands of years hence. But I have trouble believing that he could have imagined the weight of destruction a nuclear bomb might carry, for example. Thus, the philosophy of Stoicism and his meditations must be adjusted to account. So it goes for every grand idea.

Even the nuance of many lessons I am trying to instill shall one day be lost to time, with only the broad strokes remaining. Take it into yourself; keep what is useful, discard what is not, do not be bound by the wisdom of ancients who did not have the knowledge of the future.

Surely, among all the enemies you can make in this world, the foolish enemy is the most dangerous of them all. For intelligent enemies are cunning, and tactful. They will trap and ensnare you. Beguile and mislead. But at the very least, for all their deadliness, they understand self-preservation and mutual benefit. The smart foe, for all their animosity, will still work with you for personal gain. That is part of what makes them smart. They are willing to set aside their differences, and even abandon their course of action, if the threat of their own destruction is too great.

A foolish enemy has no such scruples. Either through a lack of understanding, or a lack of long-term planning, they will act according to their whims in the moment, dooming you both for their lack of foreseeing the outcome.

Imagine a swordfight between you and your nemesis. Imagine you are losing this fight, but hark, for there is a rowboat nearby. You leap upon it, and your foe follows, and together you begin sailing down the stream. You know you are safe here. This boat is rickety, and if your foe charges, even if they manage to hit you and win, the force of the weight will surely topple you both from the boat anyways, where you would drown in the deep. You have time to recover. You are safe.

Unbeknownst to you, your foe is an idiot, and charges anyways.

I remember writing about a moral aspect a long time ago for a highschool paper about the selfishness of morality; where the premise was that no action could truly be 'moral' so long as we stood to gain spiritually from it. 'You cannot act in altruism where you profit from feeling good by it'.

In this, the irony I concluded on was that only an evil person could be truly good, because they would feel nothing from this kind deed, making it a truly altruistic act.

I don't know if I believe so even still, but it's fun to think about.

Many companies, groups, and organizations will regularly oust the person who points out the problems most frequently; all the while believing that, with them gone, so too do the problems disappear; all without realizing that they just got rid of their most honest attendant.

It is strange how tolerance is so usually untolerated. When people ask for your tolerance, often what they are truly asking for is your respect, or admiration, or integration. When all they receive is your tolerance, they are not very tolerant of it.

There exists such a great capacity for selfishness, greed, and evil in this world that it can seem disheartening to even try fighting against it. What does it matter if one evil undone today just leads to another being done tomorrow. Let the world continue on. Who cares?

But listen. And know. It is *because* there are those who fight for goodness that the world continues on. It is because one truth can undo a mountain of lies, and one selfless act can topple an empire of woe, and it is these decisions, these actions, done and done again over the course of life, that allowed us to be where we are; to keep fighting, and to fight yet more.

Never give up. There is worth in the attempt alone.

There is an idea, all too frequently endorsed by those who benefit from it, that it is the righteousness of the person which decides the righteousness of the action, and not the other way around. That if a good person acts, therefore, the act itself must be good.

This idea is false, because of all the evils in the world, some of the most catastrophic were among those all too often perpetrated by those who firmly believed that they were doing the right thing.

This idea, without subtlety, without nuance, is pushed to the brink, and then we wonder why all parties seem to scramble to align themselves with the good, the just, the virtuous, all so they may commit whatever deeds they wish upon the intruder. The evil. The damned.

Since, if you are a good person, then whoever you harm must be evil. And must deserve it. Right?

There is an old Koan I once heard that tells the tale of Oda Nobunaga, Toyotomi Hideyoshi, and Tokugawa Ieyasu all sitting, drinking tea, before the chirping-song of a sparrow; whereupon it suddenly stops.

The three debate as to how to entice the bird to sing once more.

Nobunaga slams his fist into the cage and orders *"Torture it, until it has no choice but to sing."*

Hideyoshi lays bird seed at its feet and declares *"Make a deal with it, so as to arrange its singing."*

And Ieyasu lays a gentle hand on the table and remarks *"Wait, until it sings again of its own accord."*

It is through the efforts of these three traits; an iron grip, a keen mind, and a patient heart, that Japan was transformed from a land of civil strife into one of prosperity.

These qualities shall serve you too, if you can tame them.

You do not experience the world around you. Cold. Heat. Hunger. Thirst. Fear. Courage. Light. Dark. Noise. Silence. Instead, these things are experienced through the medium of your body; they make their way to your brain by way of messenger. You do not experience the world around you, but instead only experience the ways in which your body insists on reacting to them. The ways in which your mind insists on seeing them. But you are the overlord. You needn't obey these demands.

There is no true way to prevent corruption. You could devise any administration, with any level of parameters, and someone out there will find a way to skirt it, to get the rewards with none of the effort.

If something *can* be profited from, it <u>will</u> be abused for profit.

With this in mind, the solution is clear: What value system do you want your administration to hold? And how do you want that corruption to manifest in your favour?

If you cannot prevent crime, corruption, or evil, then at least organize them to productive ends.

The Pandora's Box Paradox is a scenario in which, to deter apocalyptic consequences, designers will mitigate the threshold for damage done in cases where "Pandora's Box" is opened. Ironically, this same mitigation allows people to consider *opening* the box for lesser degrees of cause.

The main example of this paradox is in Nuclear Weaponry. In order to avoid worldwide annihilation; designers of Nuclear Warheads design them to be more accurate, with fewer chances for collateral damage, and with shorter half-lives for the radiation, making them less harmful overall. But this same decision to make nuclear weaponry less destructive makes them an easier alternative to consider as an offensive or retaliatory strike than their more destructive counterparts; thus resulting in the same total annihilation the designers tried to account for.

Laws are maintained, not by the will of the administration, but the compliance of the people. There is no police force that outnumbers the people, and no jail that can hold the population. In this we see that the willingness to follow a law is what allows it to take effect.

Is it better to steal, or depend upon mercy?

There is no problem so great that someone does not benefit from its perpetuation; and those who commit themselves to stopping it often have the most reason to allow its continued existence. Even many charities and self-help centers will teach tactics and give resources that do not elevate, but martyr you (such as certain welfare centers cutting you off after you make a certain amount of money from your job, reducing the incentive to work as you make more money not doing so).

For much like a cult, these bases live and protolyze on the dime and time of the victims. (Using the aforementioned example, one could easily see that a politician making executive orders to induce poverty, and then offering aid to the impoverished, would be a fast track to reelection.)

Charities and Non-Profits are still, ultimately, businesses, and depend upon donations and kickbacks to stay active; and to gain donations and kickbacks, they must have a narrative to fulfill or push. A narrative that couldn't exist without the problem. You see how circular it is?

A hero's village may burn from dragon's fire, this is so; but it is through the dragon that they become a hero at all. What lives they lead, what riches they steal, what princesses they marry, and all because the dragon burnt their village to set them on their course. It is a short step in imagination, then, to wonder why the hero takes their sweet time in hunting the beast.

It is interesting to think that so many old ideas, those of the philosophical, ethical, or theocratic, were only accepted at the time due to the fact that there were so few other ideas LIKE them in their prime; and yet this fact doesn't make said ideas any less flawed.

In fact, it seems like a duty passed onto the students, those who love these ideas and cherish them and preach them, to come up with reasons as to why these ideas AREN'T flawed; as so many philosophies, so far down the line, have gained edition after edition, written by those who adored them, to try to patch the holes in the leaky ship they so loved; as if it were blasphemy to question if these ideas were really that good to begin with.

It is 'Determination' when we approve and 'Stubbornness' when we don't.

Corruption and tyranny often remain, to the pleasure of irony, at the behest of those who suffered under their yolk before. Totalitarianism historically persisted because with every coup, the insurgents didn't wish to tear away the bonds, but only wanted to hold them for themselves. And so the slave cannot dream of freedom where they instead dream of being the master.

"This is an affront to the gods!" cried the Paladin to the Thief.

Somehow, the Thief, who did not believe in the gods, didn't care.

The most terrible mistake one can make in any group is to make a foe out of one who means you well. The second most terrible mistake is to believe that in meaning you well, they will do you no harm.

What was once originally derived as a convenience or efficiency is, inevitably, transformed into a necessity by force of technological momentum. The greatest example of this can be seen with cars; originally a luxury, until more and more urban environments were designed around their use to the point where they become a necessity. Cellphones are in a similar boat; originally a way to maintain ease of contact, and now a necessity for any modern world where you do so much business online and so many official forms require your number. Even psychological wellness cannot escape, for in the instance of cellphones, one is always 'on the clock', and must be prepared to have their day interrupted at any moment.

On a macro level, this is reflected in the excessive, constant growth of economy almost for the sake of growth itself; as if we are but organisms within a larger host that our services allow to live for no other reason than it wishes to.

In short, what was once a luxury and convenience that was bent to serve man is often turned to bend man instead. That we must operate our lives around this technology, these cars, this growth, rather than these developments serving their original purpose of helping man achieve self-actualization.

It is terrible how much easier it is to believe your enemies wrong than prove it.

People can agree on who should run a country for entirely sensible and entirely bigoted reasons respectively; and people can disagree as to the creation of a policy where both only wish to help their fellow man. Focus less on how much you agree or disagree, and more on *why*.

Putting off a task rarely prepares one to do it the better.

Always stand by your principles, but always be aware when people are trying to use your principles against you. That does not mean that you should betray them, nor does it mean you should forgo them, nor does it mean you should change them. It simply means: Be aware.

There are those that can and will demand a certain quality and conduct from you that they would never give back in return, and it is simply because of a difference in principles that they are trying to leverage against you. How you deal with this is up to you.

To stand and run and fight may attract predators, this is true; but laying down and waiting until they pass will only attract scavengers. Between the two, is it not better to live as you ought to, with fire against the dark, than to be slain in your sleep?

Before you ask forgiveness or grant it, ask yourself: Do you desire it for your peace of mind, or theirs?

It is interesting how ideas of pride change between the classes. For the lower classes, pride often comes from 'the grind'; the idea of working long hours, usually in harsh conditions, often at the expense of one's own physical or mental health. The more hours worked, the harsher the conditions, and the more you sacrifice, the more glory is carried in the boast.

But this is not what the upper classes talk about. Those of the highest means do not sit and gossip to one another about how hard they have worked, how awful their jobs are, how much sleep they are losing, how 'on the grind' they are.

While for the upper classes, pride comes exclusively from ware and means, often inversely proportional to how hard they have worked for them; where instead of work ethic, it is cunning and opportunism that is valued and prided upon.

Not all decisions that lead to a better life are happy ones, and not all decisions that cause happiness also lead to a better life. There is a bittersweetness, and a willingness to endure even the harder days, if one is to live with the virtue and honour required for a fulfilling life in the end.

It is okay to be sad after making the right decision. There is more to life than chasing dopamine.

Pride is a virtue in its place as a steppingstone to achieve heights even greater still, rather than as a place to bed down and grow complacent.

It is strange that what is best for the individual is often at odds with what is best for society. For example, it is usually within a man's best interest to let a social or corporate problem worsen before he mends it, for if he applies preventative measures, and saves his society countless costs in repairs, they would never have realized how dire the problem was and would have given him nothing but his usual paycheck as a reward.

Yet if he allowed the problem to persist, causing high amounts of damage and costing untold amounts of money in lost opportunities, when he fixes it he would be hailed as a hero and showered with anything he desired, despite the worse outcome for not having fixed it sooner.

These kinds of contradictions often come due to conflicting interests between those who support the profitable status quo, and those who support the status quo only when it is profitable.

Compromise is often cheaper and more efficient than competition, which is exactly why you see so many monopolies to begin with.

"*God will surely punish you!*" declared the priest, as he knelt over the ashes of his village.

"*And yet here I stand.*" Mocked the bandit. "*You ask a higher power to do what you wish you could, for you are powerless. But here-*" he said, as he kicked a sword closer to the teary-eyed priest. "*If you merely picked up this sword, you wouldn't be.*"

Are you living a life worth re-living, even if nothing in it could be changed? If not, then perhaps it is you, not life, that must be different. A farmer cannot ride a gryphon when his mind is on his turnups.

It is no victory to replace a king with a politician, or a priest with an idealogue. All function requires a ruling power.

I have never seen an overbearing bureaucracy improve the lives of any citizenry. Through the whole of my life, I have learned that the main principle use of bureaucracy is to hide your own ineptitude and inefficiency behind the proxy of another branch; so that each complaint, problem, and failing can be circled around and never be anyone's fault, and that no individual must take responsibility for. If there exists any other purpose, I have yet to be convinced of it.

If Karma exists, it necessitates that whether you do something beneficial or harmful to someone, they must have deserved it. The only alternative is that blessings or curses can be made to befall someone regardless of karmic balance; in which case, having good karma obviously does not protect you from the misfortunes of life.

Yet another failing, yet another turn around the clock. It feels like history repeats itself constantly, with very little changing between each iteration. Yet time and time again people create philosophies, religions, abstract beliefs, and principles with which to guide others toward a better life.

Yet here we are, all the same.

But before judgement can be made and fostered upon any shoulders, it is always worthwhile to ask: Does the failing come primarily from the student, who listened so poorly? Who applied the lessons so naïvely? Perhaps it comes from the teachers, who's arrogance and idealism blind them to the shifting of the times. Perhaps, instead, it is the lesson itself that is failing, so unfit for the circumstances it is applied in.

For much like martial arts, they are created and honed to battle certain kinds of threats even as they fail against others. Perhaps there is no one true philosophy or religion or belief that, if accepted worldwide, would bring peace and prosperity. Perhaps that is simply not how the world works. Instead, we should treat these belief systems in the same way one treats martial arts, by applying what works based on circumstances and discarding the rest until they become necessary again.

Life is too complex for a one-size-fits-all solution. Perhaps that is the ultimate failing. Perhaps we should instead follow what mother nature and evolution has been teaching us throughout all our history; that it is not one tried and true method that works in every circumstance, but rather, that which is most adaptable that thrives.

Hypocrites have no leg to stand on, but that still does not mean the sky is red when they say it is blue.

I've never been fond of the mindset that differing ideas from differing backgrounds carry innate value to a project. Yes, a man from Japan is going to have different views than a woman from Timbuktu, but then again, so would two hundred squirrels wrapped together in a jumpsuit. An idea being different doesn't mean that idea is good, nor even feasible in your current circumstances.

It is courage to hold ourselves to the same standards we hold others.

Debt is not meant to be repaid; it is meant to be leveraged. The last thing a creditor wants you to do is pay it off; since, in doing so, they can no longer charge interest and have a lasting investment.

Likewise, so long as they are owed, those owing can rarely act against them for fear that the payments will be increased or the consequences for not paying will be magnified; and of course there is the tried-and-true method of wiping away some debt in exchange for cooperation. For many, especially in the lower and middle class of society; this creates a continuous feedback loop of working and toiling without hope of being rid of these chains.

Luckily, there is a quote by J. Paul Getty that explains a rather easy way to combat this:

"If you owe the bank one hundred dollars, that's your problem. If you owe the bank one hundred million dollars, that's the bank's problem."

In this round-about way, it is the debtor who becomes the master, as their debt is so large that their assured prosperity is the only way the creditor will ever make their money back, and so they shall go above and beyond to assist this end goal in any way possible.

(Also this is not financial advice. Please do not max out your credit cards on the hope things will go well for you.)

It is alright to call attention yourself, whether for praise or for assistance. To lump about and expect people to notice your efforts without you saying so will only tell them that you are content enough to not mind. Just as you cannot rescue a lost miner who will not cry out, so too must you raise your voice to be heard.

I have a theory that the more people you put to any problem, the more likely they are to come up with the dullest answer. The idea being that, with so many people trying to figure out a solution, they talk and squabble and bicker until they are doomed to reach the most common denominator of an answer there is.

As far as society goes; if there exists a law, so too shall it be broken. In this regard, the point of a law should not be to punish the criminal, but rather, to ensure the pointlessness of committing the crime to begin with. This is mostly impossible in civilized society, but there are great strides that can be made to diminish criminal enterprise. One rarely needs a drug dealer where they can get their drugs legally and safely in a facility designed to treat them for addiction, and one rarely needs to resort to murder if a fight to the death can be a formal affair.

In the end, all understanding is superseded by your own perception and ability to understand to begin with. You cannot understand what someone is saying if you do not speak their language, even if you would otherwise know were they speaking in yours. You require training and experience to do so. So too it is with wisdom, time, light rays, morality, and so on.

A colourblind man would not know what orange looked like, but he might be able to understand what it *could* look like if he could see the colours red and yellow side by side. Many things can only be understood if you have an anchored reference point, training, or the equipment required to filter them properly, and if you lack them, you may as well be mistaking shadows on the wall for the real thing.

The pursuance of 'More jobs! Creating jobs!' seems like a false goal if most of these jobs will never allow the population to get into an economic bracket where they can reach independence. What does it matter if you create a million jobs that pay so little you can barely afford food or rent? All you're doing is making a serf class.

If you are freed from a cage, but only under the condition that you follow the status quo lest you be returned to it, then you are not free, but only on parole.

There is a contradiction in all instruction in terms of how it plays out. My mother once told me that you could always spot the experts from the amateurs, because the amateurs tried to follow the rules to the letter whilst the experts would treat them more as guidelines. Obviously, as an amateur, you would be upset by such an act. Why should you get chastised over breaking rules that the experts are so clearly flaunting? But the punishment is not for breaking the rule, it's for not being good enough to break it.

Instruction, in general, will allow you to pursue your craft to a higher degree, but there eventually comes a time where your skill level surpasses the limits of the instruction given to you. This is why you are trained in the foundations of art before being allowed to pursue abstraction, or why many drivers, after years, will develop their own techniques that would be unsafe for a Learner to use; or as many of my blue-collar friends would put it: *"This isn't what you're supposed to do, but this is how I do it."* A master pipe-worker knows exactly how much pressure it can take before it bursts, and that's why he takes liberties with the installation. The new guy does not, and that is why he gets his ass busted when he tries to do it the same way.

If they are willing to do it to their enemy, then the only thing preventing them from doing it to you is deciding whether or not you are their enemy too.

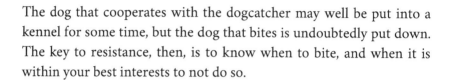

The dog that cooperates with the dogcatcher may well be put into a kennel for some time, but the dog that bites is undoubtedly put down. The key to resistance, then, is to know when to bite, and when it is within your best interests to not do so.

More often than not, the difference between courage and stupidity is in how the story ends.

Language, as a whole, is a medium to meaning. The words you are reading at this exact moment inherently mean nothing; they only have the meaning we ascribe to them for ease of use in exchange of ideas. But since not many have memorized the dictionary from end to end, most of us learn words through the context of hearing them or through others teaching us (and they probably haven't read the dictionary either); so all we're working with is implied meanings, and hoping everyone else understands.

As an example: If you and I discussed the best toppings for a 'Pie', all the while I meant the Pizza Pie while you meant the Dessert Pie, you'd be disgusted at my arguing for pepperoni while I wouldn't understand why you'd want apples on it.

Conversely, if we invented a word, "Gormgle", and we both just decided it meant the same kind of pie, the fact we use gormgle to describe it wouldn't matter. We both know what we're talking about and doing so accurately. That's the point of language in the first place.

The thing that binds most deeply is habit, not difficulty. It is not the chain that keeps us tied there, but that we stop trying to break it.

For someone who does not understand your burdens to give their opinion on how you should handle them is only worthwhile in the sense that a rainstorm is helpful in reminding you to stoke your fire. This is not to say to dismiss such opinions, as you would not dismiss the signs of a storm; but only that it comes from a place where you must provide your own kindling.

Are they evil? Or are they merely flawed? It is easy to judge as one wishes without all the twists and turns, the pushes and pulls, the leverages and emotions that may exist in one life or the next. The chronicles of the Gods of Olympus make up an epic of failure and discord; but no singular god could be labelled as evil. All they contained within them were the very errors that make up we humans, made in their image.

Poor motivations do not dismiss rational arguments. Even if someone is making an argument just for their own personal benefit, the *fact* that they benefit, or even that they wouldn't be making the argument if they didn't, isn't enough of a factor to get rid of it all together. A car salesman is motivated through personal gain. He doesn't care about the car he's selling or whether or not it will actually serve you well. He just wants his payday. That doesn't mean his sales pitch is incorrect, however; nor does it mean the car won't serve you well regardless.

It is strange how common it is that those attacking us are said to represent the whole of their sect, but those of us attacking them are only, of course, the most violent and detached minority; and do not represent us at all.

One does not need to agree in order to understand.

There is a stark difference between what is possible and what is reasonable to expect. It is always possible that you could drop dead from a brain aneurism, but it is unreasonable to live your life as if this were an impending fate. Even people who follow the philosophy of living each day as if it's their last pay their parking tickets.

What someone does is not nearly so important as how they do it.

A moth spies the full moon's silver shimmer in the waters below, and dives down to reach it, drowning in the process. If it had tried to fly up to the original, rather than the imitation, it would have fared no better a fate. And yet, ah, how much farther it would have flown.

Introspect and observe what has power and influence over you, and ask yourself why.

There is something called the "Hidden-Elephant Argument" to counter conspiracies; that basically goes:

"Why do you never see elephants hiding in the trees? Because they're really good at it."

This is meant to demonstrate how, in many conspiracies, the lack of proof can become a proof in and of itself.

This is a fine counter, and is something that ought always be kept in mind when deep diving into investigation; but it is worth noting that this counter is a fallacy unto itself, for it makes the presumption, first and foremost, that there IS no conspiracy, that elephants CANNOT hide in trees, and thus any reason why we might think there is one must surely be false; and in this sense, it is incredibly frightening to see elephants hiding atop the trees and try to point it out to someone who can perform a genuine investigation, only for them to call you mad.

Is it better to succeed at the common and mundane, or fail in the fantastical and awe-inspiring?

You build a cage to house a criminal, but once they are let go, the cage is considered a redundant space. From the perspective of the jailer, then, you catch the criminal to fill the cage.

There is no reliable way to tell what is historical truth versus what might be a less nuanced translation. The only reason we state there is a truth and untruth at all is because we have our own modern world with which to contrast it to; and since we have seen no dragons, all historical explanations of dragons must be allegories for something else.

Unfortunately, this method of reverse engineering history can very easily cause us to miss warning signs that Here There Be Dragons indeed.

On a technical level, no sacrifice is too great to protect from total annihilation. Even to give the lives of 99% of the earthly population is nothing if it prevents the alternative that everyone dies anyway.

In some ways, it is better to be found guilty of a crime than to only be accused of it; for in good society, to go to prison is seen as an act of restitution, and even the murderer is let go with some stark few sympathies of a redemptive man who has atoned.

But to be accused and found innocent is to always have a cloud over your head, that perhaps you 'could' do such a thing, and this social ostracism is your prison, and not a man in the crowd is willing to defend you lest they be accused of the self-same skeletons in the closet.

If you wish to know what benefits the people in power, look to the media. What news do they report? And what news do they not?

In an odd twist of fate, it is the fools and the perverse and the insane in the community who keep it the purest from outside influence; for it is that which is stigmatized that is avoided in polite conversation. If the gates of your utopia are guarded by the most outlandish your community has to offer, the vocal minority, then none but those who see the worst you have to offer and still remain willing to adjust to your standards will come, and those who would force theirs upon you will be turned away.

There is nothing inherently wrong with self-study or isolated research; limiting only the minor boon of your work and findings being supplemented by your peers. But this is only a boon in the way that a group of people tend to be smarter than an individual. Usually.

A poisoner is deadly, not for their concoction, but that they can get close enough to give it to you.

How many times can something be copied before the original ceases to have meaning? What meaning can be ascribed to an original that cannot be applied to a copy? I once heard this way of putting it: that if there is only one thing, then it is the best of its kind; but if there are many, even of identical quality, then the quality of them all is, by definition, average.

"Coolness" is generally subjective and seems to be in the eye of the beholder. But there are common threads that tie themes of coolness together. Authenticity, for example. Confidence. Being able to bring up the mood of those around them. Perhaps, in the end, 'Cool' is just a catch-all for someone who is happy with themselves and wishes for others to be happy with themselves too.

Any power in the universe might save you from outside injustice, or totalitarian cruelty; but the only thing that can save you from self-imposed cruelty is yourself.

Surely sacred Abrahamic texts must be, somewhere, in error. Can humans perceive perfection? If they cannot, then even if such texts were written by a perfect being, we would not be able to read it perfectly. Were they written by imperfect beings? Then surely human error must have infected the writing at some point. If a perfect being can give the ability for things to be perceived perfectly, then why are there so many arguments over scripture to begin with?

The ills of the world are not nearly so necessary as many convince themselves of. It is only a delusion, because otherwise, we'd have to admit that though we wish to stop it, we have no power to do so.

Being a victim draws the empathetic as much as it does the predatory. Power, however, draws everyone.

A quality of yours is only a fault if it gets in the way of your life goals. Do not allow someone to dictate your faults based on what gets in the way of theirs.

Just because something may have a reason does not mean it is excusable; whether it be the actions of others or in how the system operates. Everything has an origin for why it is the way it is, but ultimately, it is we who decide to keep it that way.

The greatest form of metaphysical freedom is indifference. If nobody can force you to care, they cannot force you to do anything.

The pain in a burden comes not from the burden itself, but from its lack of fulfillment. A boxer could endure a thousand punches for the prize of a championship but would not endure a single one for the prize of being insulted.

Most ills in life are social ills; caused either by a sick society or being maladjusted to society as a whole. This is often a cause for shame in many people, especially the young or the new whom had expectations thrust upon them; but shame is only true for things you yourself find shameful.

It is not anyone else's place to dictate where your dignity or value as a human being stems from. Trauma cannot take it from you, illness cannot take it from you, poverty cannot take it from you, all the opinions in the world cannot take it from you. Dignity can only ever be sold, and only for convenience.

There is no mistake so costly as the one that is not learned from.

Misery is frequently built upon a foundation of expectation rather than action. It is the player who wanted to win the most who is the most disappointed by the loss. To this end, to avoid heartache, it is best to have an ulterior motive to your actions, or a separate goal that is not conditional to things outside of your control, such as spending time with your loved ones, the glory of a job well done, or the piety of one's convictions. You cannot be that disappointed that you lost the marathon when the main reason you joined was for your health. Know this and be happier.

It can always be painful to lose someone's respect. But what do they respect? And what is that respect really worth?

It is rare for any one person to hate or love a thing in and of itself. Often, it is the associations we have with said thing that fuel our emotional attachments. Thusly, if you want to change someone's mind, focus your efforts on the association, rather than the subject.

Not every burden is a barrier. Do not believe them so.

Is darkness an absence of the aspect of light? Or is darkness an aspect in and of itself?

Be wary about the tools and resources at your disposal and keep control over your projects and ambitions. A tiger is a wonderful tool for defense, intimidation, and the herding of wild beasts; but only so long as it's not angry with you.

There is nothing selfish in claiming what is rightfully yours. But by what right *is* it yours?

There is a vast difference between dangerous and harmful. An alligator is only dangerous when your head is inside its mouth in the same way that heroine is only dangerous when it enters your veins; but only one of these can chase you.

To wait for the favour of the gods is the job of the priest.
To take it is the job of the cultist.

If something is a needle in a haystack, all the more reason to devote efforts into finding it. Even a needle can kill you if you're not careful.

It is odd that there is a stark difference between 'necessary work' and 'valuable work', since one would imagine that they would overlap frequently, yet in truth they rarely do.

A nuclear technician is extremely valuable for the work that they do, yet the guard who prevents meltdown is undoubtedly the more necessary. The most towering white collar work centers would come to nothing if they were so full of trash as to be unusable. That's why you have janitors to begin with.

The true goal of work, any sort of work, seems to be making the work itself as redundant and obsolete as possible. Crops bred to be easier to plant, grow, and harvest, for example, with as little intensive care or outside treatment from the farmer as possible. Software engineers who build machines that build themselves. Transport to take as little time 'transporting' as possible. The list goes on.

The oxymoron, then, is that many of these people's same livelihoods depend upon the existence of their work. A dentist's job is to fix teeth as efficiently as possible; but as one anonymous dentist pointed out: *"If everyone took our advice, we'd be out of a job."* This follows the logical conclusion that all workmen are inevitably at war against themselves. Tracklayers work to lay track, but once all track is laid, there is no tracklayer. Therefore, to remain employed, a tracklayer needs to lay more track, and the most efficient means of doing this is to either delay the completion of the rail or go on to make others.

Perhaps capitalism stemmed from this contradiction, so that the most efficient and fastest methods would then be rewarded rather than those that worked slower; but in our rapid economic world, crony-capitalist sentiment rewards favour and status far more than it does efficiency and workmanship. This, again, leaves the worker at war with themselves; though this time at the higher levels as well, since a C.E.O requires a problem to justify the existence of their position, and so part of their inherent job is to create problems that give rise to this need. Thusly, the world stagnates.

Which is a bit of a problem.

The perpetual motion of commerce is what keeps industry and development alive. For all the critiques one might give capitalism; that it does not allow for expansion is certainly not one of them, for expansion itself stems from a desire to accumulate yet more and more. Is the problem in the human genome then? Surely not, since not everyone is greedy, nor is every wealthy person predatory in their position. Perhaps it is no one single thing, but a combination of factors: The fear of change, fear of replacement, fear of a loss of control, so on, so forth.

In all ways the powerful attempt to keep others down and keep advancements at bay so they are not made redundant, it seems to stem less from a want for yet more power, and more from anxiety over losing what power they have. Humans are loss-oriented, after-all. To this end, if there was a way we as a society could guarantee no such loss of power and prestige, even in redundancy; perhaps through glory, or social approbation, or benefits to the industrious who came before, then there would be fewer attempts to stop the flow of the world, and more who are willing to see it through to the end.

If a secret is mundane, that only means the true secret is in the motive behind why they wanted to hide it.

The most terrible symptom of mind control is not the conscious override of rationale, but the utter conviction that you are acting of your own volition.

"*Take only two, please,*" taped to a candy bowl is a good litmus test to how shitty your children are.

Eventually, you will forget all of this. But you will remember how it made you feel. The connections you forged with the information in the synapses of your own brain.

Do not fear forgetting, for this is just as valuable as any information written herein verbatim.

WHEN I NEEDED IT MOST

Hey. This is a direct disclaimer from the author, from me to you, the reader.

This one is different from the others. It's a bit heavy. More than a bit.

If you're not feeling well, like you can't handle that kind of bitterness today then maybe it would be best for you to come back another day. It's okay. I will still be here for you when you feel ready. You have all the time in the world.

On the 21st of February, on some year that seems so long ago, I was shipped out to Quebec, Canada to complete the Basic Training course of the Canadian Forces. Though I did not graduate, coming home early, the experience itself provided many new perspectives and insights as to the workings of the human psyche, especially under stress.

. . .

Personally, I thought I did fairly well while I was there. My biggest fault being my less than perfectly clean quarters (specifically the bed, which never seemed to be folded properly).

Apparently, my platoon mates disagreed. I heard more than one unflattering comment about myself (that I should get a reward just for tying my boots right was one of them) and I will not lie in saying that it did a number to my self-esteem. My joy and enthusiasm for the experience was dwindling fast, considering I went in there expecting to do better, and so I began focusing my mind and efforts towards leadership.

Everyone got a chance as the Platoon leader in order to showcase their leadership skills, and I was convinced that while I may be subpar in every other category, at the very least I could prove myself a capable leader and not a total waste.

It did not work out.

Because of bad circumstances, bad decisions, and sheer bad luck, it seemed as if I made every mistake in the book until it culminated into me being stripped of my rank as platoon leader before the day was even over, and worse yet, the final infraction came because my pen was sticking out of my breast pocket. I was only the second in my platoon to actually lose their rank as leader in the middle of the day. And the only one of the two who took the job seriously.

It was, without a doubt, the most humiliating experience of my life.

When our and our sister platoons had first arrived, one of the things we were briefed on in the very first days of training was that of suicide and suicide prevention. In fact, we probably got more briefings upon this one subject than we had any other.

Even during the intervals between meetings we had heard little rumours about things that had happened just days before our arrival, the most prevalent being when a young man already into his release (which is the term used for when the paperwork to let them go home is in the midst of being filed) jumped out of a top story window.

No recruits were allowed onto the roof without supervision after that.

When I first heard this, I almost didn't believe it. He was almost out! Why did he feel the urge to jump when he was already nearly released? I and the rest of the platoon ended up brushing it off in that he just couldn't stand to be there any longer; yet after my own experiences, I don't believe that to be the case.

As it turns out, suicide and attempted suicide was not all that uncommon at the base, with it happening at such a rate that many isolated areas were barred from recruit entry simply because it would take too long trying to find someone who had chosen to end their life there. Recalling this now, I am almost equally surprised at the fact the instructors had such a hard time culling it. Perhaps because they never really attempted to. If you were having suicidal thoughts, you were instructed to talk to the Chaplain. Waiting times do apply.

It is odd that morale support is so lacking otherwise. Perhaps that may explain why veterans are some of the most mentally vulnerable of us all.

Don't get me wrong, I understand perfectly why the harsh and aggravating nature of military training has to remain in place. People there have to be broken down and stressed out in safe environments because they need to learn how to handle themselves outside of one. If one cannot find the hope and strength to continue on sheer force of will alone, how well could they fare in a field where people are shooting at them? Where they are cut off from supplies, friends, and communications? Because of this, 'softening' the training simply isn't an option, yet even so…

The problem is that this creates a cold-water-shock situation. Of course soldiers out in the field have to work well even when thrown into the worst of situations, but many new recruits have not experienced anything close to that; and so when they are immediately put into high-stress situations it is akin to tossing someone into a pool of ice water without allowing them to get acclimated or offer the respite of warm water every now and again, which is exactly what congratulations and recognition for good effort would hope to correct. It does not have to be accompanied by fanfare or medals or trophies just for tying one's boots, just a nod from those around you that you are actually doing well and to keep it up. Camaraderie is a big selling point of any organization, isn't it?

But who knows. Perhaps I'm just blowing hot air where it shouldn't be blown. The words of the one who failed.

It seems like people in the military are quite susceptible to mental illness and instability, aren't they? And why wouldn't they be? Going into the military is rarely a spur of the moment idea; it is only after long deliberation either as a dream job or last resort; and sometimes even a familial expectation. The point being that, for many, their career in the military is all-or-bust; so is it any surprise that they become so defeated when they are told how worthless they are? That even here at their first leap or last stop, they're a failure?

Regardless of whether someone did well or not, by withholding acknowledgement, it stops them from carrying on out of a sense of pride or duty, and twists into just trying to get through the day before their next mistake comes along. For myself, even the promise of graduation from Basic Training held no relief, because I would just be thrown into tougher, more serious situations where my screw-ups would not only affect me, but also those around me. I would go from being "The one who held everyone back," to "The one who held everyone back and got them killed," and that was supposed to be something to be excited about?

Even the idea of leaving Basic and going elsewhere had no hope in it, because why would things be different? Why would I be any less of a failure there?

You often hear of people being very confused over suicides. *"Why did they kill themselves instead of just dealing with the problem?" "Why did they kill themselves instead of just leaving?" "Didn't they see how wonderful and beautiful life is?" "Why didn't they get help?"*, to which the answers are very simple. There is no 'problem' causing them to kill themselves. There is no struggle or trial so great on its own that it defeats the human will.

It's you.

It's who you are.

Because they are the common denominator. They cannot leave themselves to make a better life elsewhere, there is no solution that they can see that would solve how the world bears down on them, there is no walk or speech or revelation that reignites the beauty of the world in the same way that there is nothing anybody could say that would make you feel *okay* after the death of a loved one.

There is no way to help them. I mean, they tried, didn't they? They tried and life smacked them back down.

How can they run from their own shadow?

People do not kill themselves because someone bullied them, they kill themselves because they realize they are *going* to be bullied, because they are just 'that type' of person and do not know how to change. People do not kill themselves because they take on debt; they kill themselves because it feels like they will never *escape* from it, from the rat race, from a system designed to squeeze them until they pop.

They kill themselves because they, as people, consider themselves a waste of skin, unfit for work or play and unworthy of living, because the very essence that combines to make them into who they are, are in themselves weaknesses of character and susceptible to suffering. That the way you feel, that loss, that agony, that despair, that sorrow so deep in your heart that it weighs your whole body down; that *that feeling* will stay with you forever.

That man did not jump from the window because he hated the place; he jumped because he hated himself, hated himself for not being the person he wanted to be, hated himself for not performing as he wanted, hated himself because if he was so terrible at something he put so much effort into, how could he ever go anywhere good in life? How could things *ever* get better?

People do not kill themselves because they are upset with their environment, but upset with themselves, and come to realize (or at least believe they realize) that in no matter what environment they are in, they will still have the same qualities that made them suffer in the first. Bad decisions, pain, heartache; these things pile on just as yesterdays pile on behind us, wearing us down into the grindstone until all we feel is hurt. Until all we ever *will* feel is hurt.

That there is no running.

No getting away from it.

That this is just how life is.

Destined to be hurt, and disrespected, and uncared for, and unhappy.

And it's not the first time either.

Statistically speaking, if someone goes to end their life, they have tried to do so before. They have felt this way before. They have felt this way for a long, long time and likely never stopped; because there is no amount of pain or suffering that ever reaches a cap, because there is no governor looking down upon the sentence of your life and deciding it's your time for good fortune. That's the gamblers fallacy. "After so many fails, I'm due for a win," but you're not.

You could just never stop failing.

. . .

I remember watching The Colour Out of Space movie with a friend of mine, and she noted that the scariest part for her wasn't the alien aspect, or the body-horror, or the rot seeping into the land, it was one moment where the farmer grabs his shotgun and turns upon his mutated animals and begins killing them, one right after the other, as he screams *"Hasn't my family suffered enough?!"*

Suffered from abuse, suffered from turmoil, suffered from not being able to make ends meet, suffered from a cancer diagnosis, suffered from being humiliated time and again as all they've ever done is try to live their lives in peace, and this was the most frightening thing because the answer is a resounding **NO**.

There is no amount you could ever suffer that would make it better.

There is no amount you could ever suffer that would protect you.

There is no amount you could ever suffer that would give you your 'due' of future prosperity. The life you deserve.

Because people don't often get what they deserve. They get what life gives them.

And sometimes you just suffer.

If whatever made this universe intended that righteousness and justice ought to be the prevailing ideals of the world, they obviously did not do enough to ensure that those following these ideals would be protected. Every day there are stories of people trying their hardest to live good, honest lives being screwed over by bad luck and ill-fortune while the scheming, cruel, and monstrous rise to the top on abuses of power and backstabbing.

The only other alternative would be that they favour evil; and looking at the world at large and historical precedent, that seems the far more likely.

A vampire flees from the sun, not because they dislike the light, but because they hold within themselves qualities that make them burn to ash when it hits them, no matter where the light may hit them, how it hits them, or why it hit them. They burn all the same.

When people with depression isolate themselves, they are not running from you, but trying to hide FROM themselves. Trying to make sure they are unseen, unheard, that maybe if nobody sees and nobody notices, they can fade away and don't have to think at all. That maybe everyone will forget they've ever known them, and they can finally fade away in peace knowing all the harm they think they've caused has been undone.

I don't think I need to tell you how well that often works out. So more extreme measures must be taken. Again, and again, and again, they try until the only way to run from their life is to end it. When you trip, do you curse the ground or your own clumsy feet? If you tripped time and again, no matter what ground you stood upon, you may not be tempted to cut off your legs, but you'd still wonder why you should have legs at all if all they do is collapse beneath you.

It is not an aggravated sense of fury at their own losses that causes hopelessness, but the perception of ALWAYS losing, and so wondering why you should even bother at all. Indeed it is so, for it is not despair that kills, but hopelessness. People do not choose to die because they have a bad day; they choose to die because they do not see themselves having any happy ones. That maybe the beauty and wonder and happiness that everyone keeps telling them about just isn't for them; as if all the dreams you've ever had for your life were able to be done, just not *by you*. Because you're not *worth it*. Because there is something in you that *failed* so long ago, before you were even born, and the rest is just you living out your punishment.

This may seem rather strange to you, but suppose you gamble or buy lottery tickets. You do so, despite the overwhelming odds you will fail, because there is hope that you will one day win. Humans can do that well enough, it is one of our best talents, to be able to continue and fight and struggle even when there is only the slightest sliver of hope. But if you did not believe you WOULD ever win... well, you wouldn't gamble, would you?

Now what if, despite not ever winning, you were still expected to play? That despite not ever winning, you saw others around you seem to win, time and again, and celebrate their winnings as they danced and sang, and you had to wrack your brain as to what could possibly be wrong with you that you just kept losing. That you saw people win and they began to look at you and mumble and groan and ask why you just *had* to keep losing, what is *wrong* with you? Why do you do this to yourself? Why are you such a failure that you can't even get *this* right? That you bought more tickets and flipped more levers and placed more bets on the roulette wheel and spun it as hard as you can and did all you could and calculated with all your brain power that if you can just win once, if you can just win once, then maybe, maybe you aren't such a failure, maybe you can do it again, maybe you can pick up here and perhaps you'll never get as ahead as everyone else but if you can just win once, if you could just win once...

And you couldn't.

This is how I felt during my time there. I truly believed that I was doing so poorly, and despite my best efforts, I would never have the time or training needed to improve myself to an adequate level. I would day-dream about graduating and being sent off on tour only to be shot and killed, WANTING to go in order to be shot and killed because at least then I would have done something right for once; dying for my country in honour and bravery; and the reasons to go back home were less and less convincing because of the very reasons I went into the military in the first place.

I did not want people to believe I was a failure, I did not want people to believe I gave absolutely everything I had only to falter, that being the showcase of what NOT to do was the best I could aspire to, because all before my date of departure I was training and researching and exercising and motivating myself and it all came to absolutely nothing. That from birth to now I had always aspired to be better than myself and never quite got past it, that my attempts were never quite good enough and always fell short, however slight, because I was a natural born failure, that was all I was, and even if it was just because of a single pen shifted slightly to the left outside of my pocket, that was all I would ever be.

Why was I put here, if only just to fail?

Why did my parents think there was anything worth having in me?

"What am I doing?"
"Why am I here?"
"Why them and not me?"
"What is my existence?"
"What am I supposed to do?"
"Is this all there is?"
"Hello universe, why am I alive?"
"Why can't I be as courageous as that man who jumped out the window?"

People will tell me that I'm here for a reason, but what reason is that? Usually it's something vague, generic, something easy to do yet unfulfillable in its totality. *"Make the world a better place."* But even so, doesn't it feel awful? Doesn't it feel miserable? To grind yourself down to a product. An effect to a cause. Let us suppose our reasons *were* achievable. And then we achieved it. What then? Do we live the rest of our life shallowly, unfulfilled, with everything we were 'meant' to do, made to do, having already been done? What's left, then?

It doesn't matter.

Grand purposes are unfalsifiable. We tell ourselves there are reasons for why things happen without ever knowing them on the sparse hope that there *being* a reason will somehow make it all worthwhile. To me it just adds to the bitterness. They say it as if there is any reason that could justify so much unfairness and cruelty in this world, from nature against man, to man against man, to man against the self.

From child soldiers to babies born with drug addictions, to happy couples being killed by drunk drivers, to crime, to poverty, to the destruction of our very world.

It's horrid all the way down.

I have sought to divine with the gods as to why this may be. If there was a sensible answer at all.

But I do not think they heard me.

We often give a sensation of dignity and honour to our suffering, in order to ease it, soften the blow. *"You will grow from this," "It all happens for a reason," "This will lead to better things," "Nothing worthwhile is easy,"* and for a time this helps. If people must suffer, why not rationalize as to why it can be a good thing? Why not give it greater dignity?

But sometimes it goes on to take a cultural shift, equating dignity with *value*, that it is GOOD to suffer. That suffering has made you a better person. As if it were a net gain. They say *"The trauma made you stronger,"* or *"You're more mature because of what you've been through,"* or supply platitudes about how much better off you are, how much more you're able to endure because of what you experienced.

I've had people tell me that they *want* their children to suffer so they do not grow up 'soft'. People who tell me that suffering makes you wise. People who tell me that it's part of a great plan; and here I think back to my poor mother who discovered her baby, dead in her crib, and screamed so loud it was heard around the block, that drove her to drug use, that drove my parents to divorce, that drove so much to ruin, and I ask if you would tell her that it made her stronger. That it was *necessary* that her baby died. That it was better this way. That it led to better things.

It didn't.

Because there are some pains so deep that you never recover from them.

We can *say* that our greatest triumphs rise from our tragedies, but this is conjecture. Supposition. Plenty of triumphs rise from other triumphs. Plenty of happy moments just happen. And that's what it comes down to. There was nothing to grow from. Nothing that made it necessary. Nothing that made it worthwhile for her child to die. Sometimes suffering just happens.

There is no dignity and honour here.

It gets a bit muddled in grey at this point, more philosophical and theoretical, wondering about the implications of free will, nature versus nurture, whether I am this way and can be changed or if I was born to be as I am with my luck as it is. Could it be said to be luck at all?

It is through these experiences that I gained the insight I did, but I gained them of my *own* volition. It was not any semblance of pain that imbued them, but the fact that I decided to *try* to learn of my own accord. That is something anyone can do, and demands no specific obstacle.

Those who want to commit suicide are not just people who lack the wisdom to try to escape poor circumstance. Nor is it a symptom of weakness.

It is a symptom of living. It can crush even the greatest of us. And has.

As someone who spent a long time wanting to take their own life, and at times still does, I'm here to tell you today that I do not know if it gets better.

I'm sorry.

I know that everyone likes a survivor's tale. I know that everyone likes those feel-good stories where someone's life is saved and they go on to do amazing, wonderful things for which they receive glory and the recognition of all their peers, having made the world a better place just like the platitudes promised, proving them right, proving that maybe suffering *is* necessary, *is* good, so that maybe their own suffering will be justified too... But that's survivorship-bias to the most ironic degree. Some people just suffer, and go on suffering, because the world can be an awful place, and the more you struggle; whether it be with addiction, or poverty, or trauma, the higher the statistical likelihood that things are not going to get better.

I'm sorry.

I wish I could give you better news.

But I am still here, as are you, so perhaps there is something to live for beyond that. Perhaps there is a reason to live, just for the sake of living, awful as it can be. Perhaps. Because sometimes just to carry on is a victory. Perhaps you will be one of the lucky few who does go on to do amazing things. Or perhaps you will just find the one thing worth living for. Or perhaps you won't.

If nobody else has told you this, then I will. You have a right to end your own life. It may sound horrific. It may sound like I'm encouraging it, but I am not. All I am saying is that you have autonomy over your own life. If there is nothing else you feel you can control, you can always control this. Nobody can tell you to go on living if you don't want to. You have the power to decide whether your life is worth living or not, and by your own standards. Not by obligations, and not by social pressures. Your reasons to go on are your own, and nobody has a right to demand you continue living for their benefit. If you do not seem to have control over anything else in life, you have control over that.

I mean... what's the alternative? What would someone tell me? *"No, they have to keep living. They have to keep living a life they hate, where they feel nothing but misery, nothing but sorrow, where nothing gets better, because if they die, it will make *my* life suck, and that's worse"*? Or maybe they will tell me that I am irresponsible for placing it in the forefront of your mind; that I should instead tell you for the one hundredth time you've heard it that suicide is a permanent solution to a temporary problem so you really should just start to feel better before you bring the mood down some more.

No. I refuse. I do not care about the hypocrisy of a culture that demands we recognize all human life as sacred and then does absolutely nothing to ensure it is a life worth living. You have control. You have the power to decide.

There are people, those who have been through it and those who haven't who will rightfully tell me that I may be crossing a boundary, but I am not addressing their pain right now. I'm addressing yours. What do they know of your pain? Your suffering? What could they possibly know, having never lived your life as you have? Just as you could not know theirs. We are all alone, and no matter how together we are in our despair, how we *feel* that despair differs. It is *you* and only you who must decide, for yourself, that it is worth pressing on. Not because of the promises another makes you, not because of a philosophy another imparts to you, but because it is your decision.

And if you are one of these previously mentioned people, those who believe I am making the wrong choice, who have known the pain that losing a loved one can bring and want to scream at me for saying all this so vapidly; I tell you that the best thing you can do right now is tell *those hurting* how I am wrong, tell *them* you are here for them, that you felt as they do, that you are there, that a life worth living is ahead of them. Tell them how you feel about them, how much they mean to you, raw, unprompted, unscripted, even if you sound stupid, even if you make a fool out of yourself, because *we are all alone here*, and it is the only thing that can convince us we're not.

Yelling at me to change my mind won't make *them* feel any better. Talk to them instead. You have the power to decide that, to save a life, of your own accord, if you want to.

And if you are one of those people who think that those who commit suicide are selfish, stupid, pieces of shit who should just pull themselves up by their bootstraps and realize how good they have it and just smile a bit more and understand that there are others who have it way worse so they ought to just suck it up; do us all a favour and *don't* talk to them. They don't need you, and you don't have the capacity to help them. What do you expect would happen if you did? That you would come to them when they're at their most vulnerable, most hurt, most in need, and pile on and make them feel even worse by telling them what awful, selfish people they are for feeling as they do? That's the pep-talk, is it?

I know you, you among these people who have had loved ones end their own lives, you too are hurting and want to lash out in a way that you feel gets the point across, but these people *aren't the ones who hurt you*, their hurt *isn't yours to feel*, and if you DO feel that loss, that sense of lost humanity from even one of us who decides it's time to check out, then actually delve into research, into the experiences of those before us, into the lives of those who hurt so deeply, and learn how to help them *properly*, so that nobody else has to go through the pain you did; and do that because if someone truly, honestly believes that the world would be better if they were not in it, trying to explain to them how selfish and stupid they are can just reinforce that idea. People who want to end their own lives already feel like complete failures. You do not accomplish what you hope to by piling on to it. What people need most is empathy, not empathy for others, but for themselves. To feel understood. To feel heard. To feel a genuine human connection. If they cannot have that with you, leave them be.

And if you are one of these others, one of those who has been told nothing but how selfish they are for feeling this way, who has read this far, then know... I don't know.

I've felt suicidal ideation for years, and never once has a day come where I am glad I did not end my own life. Where I reached an epiphany and saw the light. Every day is a struggle. And it never gets 'more' worthwhile.

But I am still here.

And so are you.

I am here because I want to be. Just as you are.

Because even if things seem without light, even if things seem without hope, we can *still* go on, even without hope. Without anything. Just because we will it.

Because just like you have the power to end your own life, so too do you have the power to continue onward. If you want to.

Of course there is always hope. People have been here, people have felt the worst of the worst life could throw at them and they carried on because they chose to. And they had happy days too, did they not? However sparse. However rare. And of course I could give any number of platitudes and meaningless quotes about the value of life or anything else you'd regularly hear from anyone else.

And perhaps I should, because I cannot offer much more.

The most I can offer you is that maybe things will get better. They haven't for me, and maybe they never will, but they *might* get better, and isn't that one day of sunshine worth a thousand days of rain? Is it not worth it to train years to be an astronaut just to take one step among the stars?

Is it not worth it to live, *just* to live? Because it is your life. So why not? You already made the decision to go this far. Perhaps I *am* wrong. Perhaps things really will get better.

And even if they do not, even if there is no sunshine, no moon, nothing but a cloudy day and the void of space, then maybe that too is enough; for even light is painful when you look directly at it. Even hope can be stifling if it is all you feel. Perhaps the resolve to carry on even without hope is a heroic act.

For all she has been through, for all she has suffered, my mother's smile still lights up the room when she sees her children. She still tells jokes. She still makes friends. She still holds grand feasts every holiday and invites all the neighbours and strangers walking down the street to come in and dine with her.

My father too, for all he has lost, for all he has tried so hard for and failed, he is still proud of what he has done, just as I am proud of him. He still plans for the future and is a respected member of his community. He is still brimming with wisdom and does not let the pain of his past get in the way of the joy in his future.

Some of my friends too, even when they feel at their worst, even when they receive the worst news, the worst diagnosis', the worse medications that kill every other part of them, they still find it within themselves to laugh and play and share and fill their home with moments of the good times.

Because there are good times.

There are wonderful, special, beautiful things in this world. And they're here for you too. Even if it doesn't seem like it yet.

And one day even I will be happy. And one day so will you.

. . .

You can take whatever you please from this essay, by no means am I to conduct what wisdom you attain from my writings. Hell, I don't even know who I'm writing it for; those who feel lost or those trying to find them. But no matter who you are, I hope you gain something.

I hope you can gain anything at all.
   So that perhaps we can all be a little less alone, together.

YOU MADE THE BEST DECISION
YOU COULD WITH THE
INFORMATION YOU HAD

*S*ome many years ago I was working with my father at the bar he managed. My duty was as a workhorse; for meager pay I would ferry boxes upon boxes upon kegs of beer and liquor between the bar itself and the shop front, as well as performing any other odd jobs from clearing trash to salting sidewalks to cleaning rooms. I was very good at it.

I wanted to impress my father and so worked as diligently as I could, helping where I was asked, and advising where it was needed, and it was very, very important for me to be correct. All the time.

Still is. So prideful am I.

So much so that at times it felt as if, if I made the wrong choice, if I were judged and labelled because of it, and if people turned to me and laughed at my foolishness, the entire ground would swallow me up and I would be unable to breathe.

Sometimes it still feels that way.

In the midst of these anxieties and in my desperation to prove my work ethic and constitution, I worked long and hard, often staying after hours with only a few other workers to ensure everything was done to satisfaction.

During one of these times, the slat door at the rear of the cooler opened and delivery men entered to exchange the now empty kegs for full ones, and as I helped them load and unload, one of the workers picked up a keg and noted that it was only half empty, and asked me, for there was no one else, what I wanted them to do with it; to take it with them or leave it there.

I thought for a moment, and knowing absolutely nothing about the process of refilling or exchanging said kegs, nor of their billing, figured that they likely wouldn't refund or scrub a half empty keg, and that my father should get his money's worth, and so I told them to leave it.

The rest of the night passed without incident, and I walked home satisfied in my decision.

The next morning, in helping my father restock the alcohol, he lifted that same keg and asked me why this one was half empty. I explained to him the situation and how I told them to leave it, and he clicked his tongue as he muttered: *"Damn, I wish they had taken it,"* and I instantly deflated.

I was apologetic, and it hurt me more than it should have to know that I had made a wrong decision. That between the options before me, I had chosen the more foolish, the more thoughtless, the more stupid, which meant I must be foolish, and thoughtless, and stupid. I felt as if all my wrong decisions were more than just an inconvenience or an unsatisfactory conclusion, and that they were, instead, a personal slight against my being. A smear. That they made me ever so slightly more unworthy of... something, anything, than I had been the day before.

Sometimes, when I cannot sleep, I still feel that way.

. . .

But in the middle of my inane ramblings, much like how I'm going on now, he stopped me, mid apology, and told me something. He told me:

"You didn't make a bad decision. You made the best decision you could with the information you had."

Then I worked my shift and went home, enjoying the walk and the time it gave me to think.

I do not believe he realized the gravity of what he said. I think, to him, it may have been a one-off, some fortune cookie wisdom to dispense when someone may be feeling insecure over their choices. Maybe he read it in a book somewhere or misremembered someone telling him something similar in his youth.

I doubt he even remembers that moment, and how it changed my life, or how I view it.

"You made the best decision you could with the information you had."

I spent the next seven years thinking about that. Quizzing myself on it, seeing how well it held up to scrutiny. Playing with it, thinking it over and seeing the shapes it could take as if it were clay, and when it hardened and set too much for my liking I would break it back down to its components and begin anew, to see what else it could apply to. I've told it to countless people when they were going through hard times, uncertain over their decisions, what the future may hold, or especially when the guilt of failure wracked them.

When someone made a call that had irreversible consequences.

Economic hardships.

Personal loss.

The death of a loved one.

· · ·

Something I learned very quickly was that people have a tendency to pass judgement in retrospect; with all the context and conflicting perspectives that different viewpoints provide; context and viewpoints that those making the decision may not have been privy to.

We judge things like intellect and wisdom by its results rather than the forethought that went into those decisions in the first place; and we are very eager to make those judgement calls in a wide brushstroke over the individual and all events they faced, perhaps because it is easier than picking it apart piece by piece.

But people are more than the culmination of their choices, I think; and a man's taste is not defined by meals he has eaten in poverty.

But perhaps I am mistaken. It is true that smart people tend to make smart decisions, and stupid people tend to make stupid ones; and so perhaps it is completely fair to judge based on results. Perhaps it is completely fair to strip Publius Quinctilius Varus of all honours and dignities for his greatest failing, The Battle of the Teutoburg Forest, and move on as if the judgement alone carries the full weight of truth; so let us judge him once more here, and see what verdict is given.

Varus, as I will now be referring to him, was a Roman general and politician living under the reign of Emperor Augustus the first who ruled from 27 BC to 14 AD. For a total of four years, Varus governed the Roman province in Africa, then Syria, where he was known for his harsh and decisive rule, before returning to Antioch where he was appointed governor of the newly established province of Germania.

As he was preparing to march to his winter headquarters with his three legions, Varus was told by Arminius, who was a German Prince and a hostage to Rome in order to secure loyalty, that there were revolts being sprung in the West and that he ought to go put them down. Varus agreed, waving off warnings not to trust Arminius, and rushed his troops to squash the rebellion.

Unbeknownst to Varus, there was no rebellion. Arminius had been plotting against him for some time, uniting tribes to his banner with the intention to annihilate this Roman army.

Three separate times the Roman army had been ambushed as they went further west, and yet they pushed on, further and further, until they arrived at Teutoburg Forest; and as they nervously trekked through the thick brush of the dark woods they were ambushed for the last time. Stones and spears were flung from behind the trees in volleys so thick that the Romans had to press all their muscle behind their shields for fear of having their skull crushed, and the clamor and clanging of stone against metal was so fierce that they could not hear the steps of the Gallic warriors pouring out from the dark until they were already completely overrun by the furious defenders.

It was a slaughter. In the midst of battle, Varus, seeing the blood and gore, hearing the cries of agony in his own tongue, and seeing his men desperately trying to flee for their lives only to be cut down, knew that all was lost; and took his own life by falling on his sword as was the Roman custom.

Twenty thousand men were lost in this expedition, including five thousand of them being hosted by these same feigned allies, who had been killed in silent raids while they slept.

The news of this titanic loss of men would cause the normally level-headed and wise Emperor Augustus to be driven to near madness, ripping at his hair and bashing his head against the walls of his palace as he cried: *"Quinctilius Varus, give me back my legions!!"*, and the serial numbers of the battalions slain would never again appear in the Roman military; thought to be an ill omen and bad luck.

Varus' political legacy in Rome was completely washed away, along with the aspirations of his son, now doomed. All those who had recommended Varus or otherwise had positive associations with him were put under severe scrutiny; some losing everything, and others sacrificing scapegoats just to stay afloat; and monuments bearing Varus' face had it scrubbed away.

This defeat had crushed any dreams of spreading the Empire further into Germania, and Varus' very name became associated with catastrophic failure.

This, 'The Battle of Teutoburg Forest', is recorded as one of the worst Roman defeats ever suffered, and the whole of the blame rests squarely upon Publius Quinctilius Varus.

Because he was a catastrophic failure, and it is so easy to see why.

It is so easy to blame him for being so eager to crush a revolt that it can be easy to forget that he was given a direct order from his Emperor to expand Roman influence and consolidate power, and that he may have seen this as an opportunity to do just that; and that not doing so would be against the will of the Emperor. Not to mention that if he allowed a revolt to simmer over the many months of winter; it could become yet another costly war.

It is so easy to blame him for a lack of preparation and the underestimating of his foe that it can be easy to forget that nigh everyone, from all generals who had surveyed the area, right up to high political figures in the capital of Rome, had declared that Germania had been successfully pacified and was fully committed to Roman rule.

It is so easy to blame him for trusting the betraying Arminius that it can be easy to forget that Arminius, for most of his life, had been an astute Roman citizen and even a Cavalry Auxiliary in the military. In fact, he served with distinction during the Great Illyrian Revolt and had been Romanized to the point where many Gallic Chieftains initially distrusted him, and that both the faction he was born from and his own brother were completely loyal to Rome, fighting against him in the coming wars.

It is so easy to blame him for dismissing the warnings about Arminius' treachery that it can be easy to forget that Segestes, the man who bade this warning, held a grudge against Arminius and had motive to lie, and who's reputation was likely not known to Varus, who would have thought of himself as protecting and standing up for one who had, up to this point, served loyally and diligently with no cause for suspicion.

It is so easy to blame him for pressing on, despite the frequent ambushes he faced, that it can be easy to forget that not only was he being called to crush a rebellion, but to assist newly formed allies of Rome; allies who may be depending upon them, that Roman honour insist he help them, no matter the cost; and that if he had left, and turned around, he could have easily been leaving them to die.

It is so easy to blame him for not sending out a damn scouting party at the very least, and for rushing so headlong into shoddy terrain rather than planning covert strikes or counterattacks, that it can be easy to forget that such measures weren't commonly taken by Romans, who preferred open battle and who's tactics generally leaned toward defense and attrition. Who considered such scheming military maneuvers as cowardly and 'unbefitting' of Roman dignity.

It can be so easy to blame him indeed.

But now I ask you this… Suppose Arminius *was* loyal, and not lying. Suppose a rebellion really was occurring. Suppose his allies truly needed his aid and that without them, Roman trust, influence, trade, and all that was so needed to consolidate a new province would fall.

Suppose, then, that he did not go. Suppose what we would be saying about him now, and how he had let all of Rome down.

Supposing things had just been a little different. Would he not be making the right decision to go?

And suddenly it is not so easy to tell.

Poor Varus. Poor stupid, worthless Varus, who's greatest misfortune was that his post was not taken by another; another who was nigh certain to have made the exact same decisions he had, so much were they a product of their time, their training, their culture, their experiences.

. . .

It can so easy to place blame and cast judgement in retrospect for the exact same reason that it is so easy to cast it upon our past selves; as if they were just us, with all the knowledge we had now, as if they had placed all bets upon red when the wheel came up black, as if they should have known, they should have known, **you** *should have known…*

But how could you?

There is a comic artist somewhere on the internet who goes by the handle 'Shen'. I don't much read funny pages, and so these kinds of comics never appealed to me, but there is one of his I saw that did, very much.

And much like the words of my father, I do not know if he understood the full weight of what he was saying when he first made the comic for the punchline.

In the comic, which I have always called *"That Dice Roll"* comic when talking about it with others, he talks about how people often equate a bad outcome to a bad decision, but that this isn't necessarily true. Sometimes you can put a lot of forethought and planning behind a decision and still be tossed onto the rocks by a storm appearing out of nowhere.

He demonstrates this by referring to a gamble, a roll of the die; that you roll a single die and you can bet that it will either land on the face of the 1, 3, 4, 5, or 6, OR you can bet that it will land on 2, and 2 alone; and that, obviously, all things being equal, it is sensible to take the first option. You have a higher likelihood of winning.

It is the sensible option. It is so sensible that most people I have asked have presumed that it's some type of trick, that they would get more betting on the two, or that it was a loaded die, but there is no trick question, there is no secret, there is no extra glory or reward for taking the extra risk. It is objectively the smart decision, the wise decision, the right decision to take the first choice; and in a life so full of variables, so full of self-doubt and hidden context, it can feel odd to talk of anything in such certainty; that it is the right choice to take the first option.

It is the right choice.
Of course it is, it always was.

But it can still land on 2, can't it?

"Just because the outcome was unfavourable doesn't mean the decision was flawed"

is the text that appears right before the punchline.

There's something strange in that. Like when I read it, I lose a part of myself. Like there is some light drifting off into a void that can be neither mastered nor shaped. A void of luck, chance, fortune, and misfortune.

There's another quote just like it that gives me the same feeling, when Jean-Luc Picard says:

"It is possible to commit no mistakes and still lose. That is not a weakness. That is life."

Poor Varus. Poor foolish, naïve Varus, who's greatest misfortune was being born into a world where such a thing is so utterly and resoundingly **true**; and such poor, foolish we, who can do nothing but sit and look back and think on how stupid we all were for being blown in the winds of fate's whimsy.

How stupid we all are, for not knowing; for acting and deciding and declaring without ever knowing the ending before it has come, as if we **ought to**, as if we *should have*, as if we could have read all the way to the end as if it were spoilers in your favourite book, and we just *chose* not to.

What a misfortune it is to be born into such a world, where you could make that bet and lose and know that a thousand years into the future people will still be looking back at you and laughing and talking about how you so clearly should have known the die would land on 2.

That it is your personal failing that you did not. That you should have just been blessed with precognition. That you should have just been anyone but who you are. That maybe you should have just thought a little bit harder before you chose to be born.

What cold reasoning. What Machiavellian reasoning. The same Machiavelli who is nigh sanctified for his wisdom in the art of statecraft and politics, whose very name is associated with cunning and guile. The same Machiavelli who, in his life, endured more defeats than he ever tasted victory, whose legacy was not even read by those in his time. The same Machiavelli who seems so clearly a master and yet suffered as if he were not, for perhaps it is true that just because the outcome was unfavourable doesn't mean the decision was flawed.

It's not a personal failing that you were unlucky. Ill-fortune does not make you more unworthy than you were before. Chance does not place a smear upon your soul. You made the best decision you could with the information you had; in such a frame where you were, a product of your time, your culture, your mind, your experiences, your perspectives.

It is not your fault you were born. And you can still make the right choices just as you are.

I will end this on a silly note, with the scenario that got me thinking on all this to begin with.

I was playing a videogame, an online top-down multiplayer shooter, and my team and the enemy team were neck in neck.

The timer ran out, and big bold words flashed across the screen that the team who got the next kill got the win.

Me and my team were hiding in an enclosed room, waiting for the enemy to come in and get us for an ambush. But they were sly; they gathered around the door and booted it open, throwing a pile of grenades into the room.

In this instant, as I was closest to the door, my mind ran through with a scenario. That if the grenades exploded upon us in this tight, enclosed room, and someone didn't get out of the way fast enough, we would lose.

But if I could burst through the door and shoot one of them down right before they went off, when they weren't expecting it, I could get one of them before the grenades brought us down and score a win for my team (It is worth noting that I had never played with these gents prior, and so couldn't judge the skill of any; and only had a fraction of a second to run this through my head and decide).

I made my choice. I burst out of that room guns blazing in every direction; probably shouting in real life as much as in-game; as all my foes were taken aback, either rushing behind cover or trying to shoot me down first.

The grenades hit the ground as my team darted every which way they could to try to evade the frames of damage and prayed that their internet wouldn't lag and get them caught in the blast.

I shot until my entire clip was empty.

And the grenades went off.

Killing nobody.

While I stood outside.

In full view of my foes.

And got absolutely riddled with bullets.

I died, and my team lost.

Anyone who's ever played a competitive multiplayer game can tell you just how much I was raked through the muck in that moment, both by my team and my enemies. It is made all the worse for the fact that I was trying to advise them on tactics throughout the match and got it flung back in my face for not following my own advice and I tried desperately to explain that just because the outcome was unfavourable doesn't mean the decision was flawed but they just called me a fag and T-bagged my corpse. It was horrible.

I admit that I left. Not out of anger, but out of shame; that I let my team down. That I was an idiot, a fool who had made such a terrible decision. Would they?

I have made so many wrong choices throughout my life. I have done so many things that blew up in my face or hurt the ones I loved or just make me squirm when I think back on them. The awkward silences and all the attempts that fell flat.

It is so easy to just want the earth to swallow us up. To never have to worry about whether or not we'll make those bad choices again.

And it is difficult, when we're kept awake on those cold nights, to decide what we could have done better. That there really is anything we *could* have done better if the difference between the right and wrong decisions are encompassed solely within the skill of the one who makes them, and the fortune that presides over them.

That maybe, perhaps, we did not make a wrong decision; but only made the best decision we could with the information we had.

And, sometimes, on those late nights when those old memories of missed calls and misjudgments keep us up, perhaps that thought alone can help us sleep.

UNDERSTANDING

*W*hy do people act as they do?
Regardless of what you answered, this essay will continue.

When you ask such a question, you have to think about both <u>what</u> they're doing, and what they're *trying* to do. For, unfortunately, these can often be two very separate things.

People are rather dynamic and are as unique as the circumstances we find ourselves in, so the ideas in this essay will be regarding empathy.

(Disclaimer: This, of course, does not include all people. I am well aware certain people cannot be grouped under the same reasonings that I am giving, but so long as you accept that this is the over-arching principle, or at least the majority thought process, we can move on just fine).

To start with, there is a grave misunderstanding of what empathy actually is. It is not *"how would you feel if it happened to you?"* but *"How would you feel if you lived their life, their experiences, had their values, AND it happened to you?"*

It is the process of seeing someone else, not as a reflection for your own traits or how you would act, but as their own individual; with their own thoughts, feelings, wants, and worries. If you offered an impoverished person charity and they reacted extremely harshly, far more than is truly reasonable, you would get nowhere asking yourself: *"How would I feel if I were being offered a hand-out?"* You must instead ask: *"How would I feel if I were looked down on my whole life and people thought I couldn't do anything on my own, and I was THEN offered a hand-out?"* and when phrased thusly, the justification for the reaction is more understandable.

Indeed. Their reaction. Because when you lash out at someone being rude to you, you are not lashing out at the individual so much as you are the essence of rudeness. When you get frustrated with a server who takes too long with an order, it is not the individual that earns your scorn, but the time that was wasted. Most everyone else reacts the same way. They are not reacting to *you*, but the essence of your words, your actions, your behaviour. They are reacting to what it represents for them. People respond to *associations*, what they *believe* something *represents*. The crux of empathy, then, is seeing through their eyes. What does it represent *to them*?

There is this anime I really like, *'Sayonara, Zetsubou-Sensei'*, which covered this exact issue in a round-about way, where it explained that when you make a joke about someone's silly name, you find it funny because you've heard it just the once, while they are snappish because they've heard it a thousand times. In this it is shown more clearly: They are not angry at the joke, but that they've heard it so often. They have an association with it that you do not share, and must stretch your empathy to be able to understand.

This is why it always tickles my funny bone when I try to encourage that kind of empathy; of understanding toward someone else's struggles, and the response is *"Well if it happened to me..."*

But it's not happening to you. It's happening to *them*. How do *they* feel about it?

It is unfortunate that so many seem unable to parse this.

I covered this subject with a friend of mine, and for argument's sake, some of her responses will be included herein as follows:

"Call me a shameless optimist but it seems such a correct view to have (that compassion and empathy are already the guiding line of all social interaction) that your insistence that others don't share it vexes me. Even if you might be right, it just doesn't make sense to nitpick."

Of course it doesn't, and of course she was right, but oftentimes the way we feel about things *doesn't* make sense, nor do the reasons behind them. Most people don't even know *themselves* very well; and the distance between who we are and who we imagine ourselves to be is often greater than it is lesser. Our scope of understanding toward *ourselves* is already narrow, much less toward anyone else. And that makes the gaps between identifying with others all the wider. It should come as no surprise, then, that most people have a hard time seeing things through the lens of others' viewpoints.

"But isn't it just basic compassion? Isn't that required for a society to run?"

I suppose that depends on the state of the society. In most every study under the sun, the findings are unanimous; that the more strife and hardship there is, the more likely people are to become selfish and callous. The worse we feel, the worse we tend to treat others. This isn't even accounting for the fact that most people do not wish to be compassionate toward those they dislike, nor do they want to be compassionate when they feel cheated, or when they feel owed. There is little compassion spared to our tribal opposites. To strangers. To those we believe are opposed to us.

"But why not, God-Emperor Cue who is so perfect and handsome and is also super good at cooking no matter what anybody says?" (paraphrasing).

Because they believe their compassion is unappreciated, that certain people do not deserve it, or that certain people have even taken their happiness. They feel as if they "worked hard enough", and so have a right to be owed something and get more frustrated when they receive nothing. Take any protest movement, for example. You could ask any of the protesters to have compassion toward the affiliates they are protesting against but many of them would hate you for so much as suggesting it; because to them, these affiliates represent everything that made their life miserable, whether or not that's true is irrelevant to how they *feel.*

"But life isn't just a movie and everything isn't split into heroes and villains!"

Whether or not life is split that way is irrelevant. It's how it *seems* to be split that matters to the common man.

Someone can only see things from their own perspective, and that's not a flaw, that's just a fact. They are the protagonist of their story and anything against them is the antagonist. That's why people almost revel in the idea of being the underdog; why you see people who almost seem like they WANT to suffer, who do so little to improve their circumstances, because it is validating. It is why there are so many who only want an opponent or force or ideology they can just punch out and be done with it rather than approaching the problem with the nuance it deserves.

Look at politics. Religion. Social policies and the debates that rage from them. Economics and its role in the fate of our world. It seems as if everyone is angry, eager to get at eachother's throats; eager, even, to hate and destroy. It certainly *seems* that way. Even if it's rarely true. But in the face of what it seems, whether or not any of these things are really true doesn't matter.

"But what about empathy? What about love?"

The answer remains the same, love and empathy often fail because to many it is more important to be right and win than it is to find the truth. People burn bridges, end friendships, even tank economies all because they want to win. If these problems ended, they would only find others; and they do this because *fighting* a problem is easier than *solving* it; and if there is any problem that is said to be solved by a wide, sweeping one-two punch policy, it is a problem that is being oversimplified.

And that often doesn't bode well for personal fulfillment. Or victory, for that matter.

To make matters worse, when pushed into a corner, people often use every excuse in the book to justify why they are not responsible for their own actions, and that someone else is to blame for 'causing' their reaction. That the sinner is not he who acts, but he who causes the act.

There is no compassion or empathy because, in their minds, they're not fighting people, but an ideal. When someone says: "all men are pigs," they're not actually saying it to their little brother whom they love dearly, they're speaking of an imaginary figure. When someone says: "all Muslims are terrorists," they're not saying it to their co-worker who they covered multiple shifts with, they're saying it to the representation they have in their head. When someone says: "all jocks are stupid," they're not saying it to a sports-loving friend they respect, they're saying it to a stereotype. Because they imagine a group, and present the group a certain way, it becomes difficult to foster understanding between *any* party, and even harder to understand the effect such presumptions have on those around them.

A white man strolls downtown yelling about how blacks are all violent; a black person, having a horrible day and lacking the patience, punches him in a rage. The black person feels he deserved to hit the man because he had suffered much that day and the man was being vile and deserved to be hit. In his mind, he did not punch the man, he punched what the man represented: bigotry. All the while, the white man doesn't even realize that people are mad at him because of what he's saying. They didn't punch him because he was angering them, they punched him because he was right and they were all violent, so on, so forth.

"But God-King Cue!" you're forced to shout up at me because I am on a plateau leagues beyond anyone and anything that will ever be. *"My [X specific group] are not extremists at all! We are doing the right thing, always! And among the extremists we have met within our group, they are still more kind and reasonable than the extremists of THEIR [Y specific group]!"* and I am very glad you pointed that out, strawman. You really are my favourite. For lo, I will now explain to you why you feel that way; and it is because of in-group bias.

"We judge ourselves by our intentions and others by their actions," is a quote attributed to... multiple people at this point, but I find it to be consistently true. I would even go a step further and say that where we judge ourselves by what we *hope* to do, we judge our foes by what we think they *might* do. The people around you, even the extremists of your group, agree with you for the most part. And since you are a reasonable person, surely they must be reasonable too, for the most part. But since those fellows over there are your foes, who *disagree* with you, why they must be very unreasonable indeed. In fact, *since* they disagree, they must either be stupid or malicious, and their extremists doubly so.

. . .

"But Your Majesty! You misunderstand!" (I scoff, beyond your earshot, as if there were anything beyond the scope of my massive brain) *"X specific religion/economic view/political view/social view actually changes real world events! And hurts genuine, real people through their lack of insight and foreknowledge! As a result, it is my duty to hate them and fight against them with all my might!"* to which I respond: **Is** *that* <u>so</u>?

When the 14th Dalai Lama, Tenzin Gyatso, heard of the Chinese soldiers destroying Tibetan temples and slaying his people, all because they believed they were doing the right thing in stamping out these monks and 'unifying' their nation, he did not hate them. He only pitied them at worst, and accepted it as fact at best; that these people, deluded as they were, truly believed their carnage was assisting their cause. It was a reflection of a toxic ideology, not of them. He believed that these people could be reasoned with, that they were still his brothers and sisters under the sun and continued to reach out his hand in cooperation toward them. What threats are you facing that are so vast that you have no opportunity to try reasoning with the perpetrators?

"Cue. Though your arguments are sound, there is still the fact that, even if I do not personally suffer, or our suffering is not so immense, people are still suffering over unfair and unjust reasons."

Of course I am not saying that just because you may not personally suffer, or because the suffering of your in-group may not reach some arbitrary 'suffering meter', that you should let evil and injustice run rampant. What I am saying is that it *will* run rampant for as long as violence begets violence, and as long as you insist that others should suffer as you have.

It is unfair to ask of anyone, and yet someone must bite the bullet and accept the short end of the stick to stop the constant cycle of hatred that flows from one person to the next. Like generational trauma, we must decide that the pain stops with us, lest we devolve into the same barbarity that destroyed so many of the Hatfield's and McCoy's so long ago.

To live properly in a social world, we must develop empathy; and we cannot develop what we do not practice. Start by realizing the truth that things are rarely as morally black and white as they first appear. In talks on writing fiction and analysis, Ben Bova, a brilliant writer whose name is one letter away from being hilarious, has this wonderful quote; and it is wonderful because it applies to the living world as much as it does the fantasy. It goes:

"Every tyrant in history was convinced that he had to do the things he did for his own good and for the good of the people around him. [...] There are no villains cackling and rubbing their hands in glee as they contemplate their evil deeds. There are only people with problems, struggling to solve them."

This is what you must keep in mind when dealing with individuals; whether they be friends or foes, helpers or hinderers; that they are rarely wholly good and wholly evil unto themselves, but that they are only reacting to the problems they perceive in their life. Their problems, however trivial they may be from your perspective, are still real to them. We mock children for getting upset at the silliest things only to think back to our own childhood, our own horrible memories of people treating us callously or saying cruel things to us because *they* thought *our* concerns were silly too. Do not perpetuate this cycle. Think from the perspective of the person you are dealing with. What do *they* want? What struggles are *they* facing? What anxieties do *they* have?

When you understand this, you can go on to the second step. You *talk* to them. Not shout at them. Not try to bend their arm until it breaks. Seeing someone either as a tool or a nameless henchman for a higher order will prevent you from seeing them as what they are: a person. A person with thoughts and feelings, memories and a life, dreams and desires, no less complex and real than yours. Addressing these concerns, these feelings, rather than trying to diminish them, trying to tell them that what *they* feel is not as important as what *you* feel will only back them into a corner. It will resolve nothing and make both your lives harder. Even if your concerns are right, true, virtuous, honourable, whatever trait you like to attach to yourself to justify your dominion, *if you are an asshole about it, nobody will want to listen to you*. You are not obliged to give everyone respect, but you will find that offering even a little bit of dignity and sympathy will go a long way to receiving it in turn.

Most people are just scared. Even the type of people who scare *you*. Because life is terrifying and uncertain and random, and we are all just trying to deal with it in any way we can. Most people just want to feel like they make a difference, and they want to feel like they are important. They want to feel safe.

Think as they do, from their perspective, without diminishing them, without presuming that they're just malicious actors or naïve moralists. Think of *why* they would want the things they want without assuming the worst *or* best of them, and what experiences in their life informed the solutions they came to. You won't be able to convince them of anything else until you do.

It's not about winning or losing. It's about understanding. The sooner you understand, the sooner you meet the person you are battling, rather than the ideal behind them.

And isn't the point of the battle to make a better world to begin with?

What a wonderful world it could be if we tried.

BUSINESS AND MANAGEMENT

"The way to become rich is to put all your eggs in one basket and then watch that basket."

   - Andrew Carnegie

---

*H*aving a good business and doing good work is about more than just being good at what you do, it's about being true to it; having your energy and will focused upon it like a pin, being able to make sacrifices of time and luxury, and putting a piece of your life into what you do; because that's exactly what your work is, a reflection of your passion.

It is unfortunate, then, that nearly everyone seems unfulfilled by the work they do and with good reason. Effort that seems without result is poison to the soul. Conversely, even the most pointless of tasks can be fulfilling if people feel it has a direct impact on the world around them. This is why many workers take the most satisfaction, not from the work itself, but the idea of helping people. It is also why you *must* be passionate about the company you set out to build. A lack of enthusiasm and knowledge both will cause negligence and mistakes.

If you build with a mind to wealth, you may achieve success, but to build with a mind to make a *difference* will give you wealth alongside peace of mind and a duty that energizes instead of diminishes you. That is why most every business mogul and tycoon always recommends putting your efforts and wealth into *only* the endeavours you care about, because a lack of care will lead nowhere good.

Now onto the actually useful stuff. The two main principles for prosperity are: Expand slowly and take on little debt. If you expand too quickly, you are likely to suffer the teething pains that come from an economy unprepared for it, and if you take on too much debt you are likely to be too constrained to overcome the next issue you'd need a new loan *for*. Many businesses have failed because they ignored one, and often both, principles. So long as these are held to and you are already filling in a market niche and making a reliable income, your prosperity will only increase from here. Most any other law is just salad-topping.

The niche bit is important though. Broadly speaking, the key to revenue is in finding the niche that offers it. Following the 80/20 rule of the Pareto Principle, the vast majority of your profits will not come from an expansive business, but rather, repeated, loyal customers who happen to be really into whatever you have to offer. This is why, as tempting as it may be to branch out to net a wider market, you must think very carefully before doing so, without letting greed cloud your judgement. If you branch out too much, it may dissipate the very niche that gives you those loyal customers to begin with. Furthermore, one of the main benefits of sticking to a niche is that you do not step into the territory of other corporations and businesses to become a competitor; and they, in turn, stay out of yours. Fierce competition is proven to be excellent for innovation and creativity, but is a terrible drain on resources nonetheless. Choose wisely before you feud.

That being said, do not get stuck too deeply into your niche either. Expand into it, and if your niche is restrictive, accept that your business might have to be satisfied with never being a nation-wide name. If you are a business that specializes in selling old games, for example, you must change and flow with the times as to what an 'old game' is and be willing to market those products alongside those you originally started with. Always remain innovative, and take advantage of changes of changes to the market and society you live in.

Not to say your business model should necessarily change, but that the way you operate it should flow with the times. Many businesses fell because they stubbornly stuck to an outdated system, whether it be not adapting to the internet and utilizing it as another resource, or something as simple as not seeing the value in delivering goods. Remember that a convenience unfulfilled is a reason the customer should choose the competitor.

If you want to branch off into a different product, the best strategy is often just making a different brand to go with it. Better to have your brands simple and numerous than complex and few. The reason you'd branch off into separate, simple brand rather than to consolidate all services into the same brand is because it is easier to change the nature of your business than it is to change the customer base. Customer loyalty is a big deal. A VERY big deal. People are creatures of habit and like associating themselves with certain brands. Sports advertising plays into this perfectly.

Therefore, before you move forward in any business venture, your first and foremost decision should be to decide on what customers you want to attract. This is also why location is a big deal. Certain clientele, whether in regard to leisure or commerce, will congregate in certain areas; and if you base your business around a clientele that is unavailable (such as a clothing store in a nudist colony), you will be shooting yourself in the foot.

Once you decide on your path, you must either lean into it heavily or depend well on your first-time customer loyalty (which is also why many pubs will offer a free first round during tourist season, or why many sit-down restaurants will offer a free appetizer or meal for special occasions. It is there to create the hook in your mind that "the pub" is that one specific designation, and "going out for your birthday" means going to the same place to get a bite to eat).

Know your customers well and treat them well, lest you alienate both the potential customer for trying to appeal to them too much and the existing customer for not appealing to them at all. Only appeal to a new demographic when you have a new business, and when planning on opening new businesses, even simple ones, it is nigh always better to open conservatively and of consistent quality and placement, based on information you know is good, than to try to expand as rapidly as possible into areas of lesser quality and placement, all on shoddy information, and being unable to recoup the costs. It is easier to accrue wealth than it is to get out of debt; and if missing a couple opportunities *keeps* you out of debt, it has already made you wealthier thereby.

I know that it is tempting to want to get in before a market becomes saturated; and this is especially true with heavier competition since it's rather difficult to copyright a niche but know that biting off more than you can chew just means that you'll choke, and your competitor will win in the end anyways. Do not let yourself make the mistake thousands of businesses have already made for you. Even in matters of potential profit, it is better to go slow. A consistent, reliable cashflow is better than huge lump sums some months and nothing the next. Consistency and reliability are the lifeblood of industry, in everything from the quality of the product and service to even the quality of management and upper brass, and the more stretched you are, the more even minor hiccups can spiral out of control.

. . .

Arguably, it is better to focus on optimizing what you have *before* expanding, so even if the expansions fail, you still have something reliable to fall back on; and when laying a proper, reliable foundation, there is no better than the simple satisfaction of your workforce.

It should go without saying the importance of fairness and happiness among your employees, but unfortunately, it cannot. The morale of your workers is paramount to your success; both because a happy employee is more productive and pleasant than a frustrated one, and because worker loyalty will ensure that your skilled, talented employees stay to move up the ranks and improve your company instead of taking your training and leaving the moment they can. You want to keep your employees happy? It is no different than keeping your company efficient. The best thing to do is simply ask them what they would like to be happier. For some, it is increased pay. For others, it is more creative freedom. For others still, it is having more meta-rewards like being able to use their remaining hours for play if they complete all their work before the deadline, or scholarships, or medical benefits.

Treat your managers no differently. Heed the Peter Principle. People should not be promoted based on time worked, or even skill demonstrated in their current field, but due to skill and understanding of the field they are trying to reach. Perhaps most importantly, they should be promoted because they *want* to be, not for added benefits that come with the position, but because they desire the responsibilities of the position itself. This is also part of why it's important to treat your employees fairly and with adequate rewards, so they do not feel pressured to climb a ladder they are not qualified for. Do not be afraid to devote a hefty portion of profits to keeping workers happy and healthy. Spending money to make money is a common saying in business, but somehow it is imagined that this only applies to raw goods and opening new locations rather than caring for the employees that make it all possible.

Even regarding direct management, a very common problem

clogging drains and interrupting the flow of industry is administrative overreach. The man to talk to about problems at the farm is the farmer, not the man who makes the tractor. Be rid of rigid oversight, simply ask your subordinates, whether they be franchisees or employees, what would make their job easier. What problems they identify as getting in the way of the business. Ironically enough, most employees regularly report that it is the manager themselves that gets in the way, with a 2012 Forbes poll showing that 65% of workers would rather have their boss fired than take a pay raise. Do your business a favour and let them work. Goodness gracious, the whole point of franchising and hiring is to be able to let go of the reigns and allow other people to worry about how to handle it; so why ruin it by tightening a leash?

And speaking of administration, it is nigh always preferable to think long-term than short-term, which on the surface seems obvious, but in practice is more difficult to get through. It all harkens back to the marshmallow test. *"The Marshmallow Test"* refers to the Stanford Marshmallow Experiment where a group of children were given the choice between the reward of either a single marshmallow right away, or two marshmallows if they were able to wait a period of time before receiving it.

In follow-up studies of adolescence and mid-life, it was found that the children who were able to wait had consistently better qualities of life than those in the first group, and though this study has since been challenged (showing the key role that economic background can play), it is still significant that 'up to half' of the measure of quality of life came from the ability to delay immediate gratification in deference to greater rewards in the future. Resist the urge to cash out and splurge. Resist the urge to count your chickens before they're hatched. Instead, push the flow of profits back so that most of it serves the very business that makes it for you. Expand. Add benefits. Double the marketing budget. *Always* double the marketing budget. If you spend money on something that doesn't directly serve the business, you are cutting into your future profits.

And please, for the love of all the divine, do *not* cut corners to save profits. Learn from the mistakes of companies like BP and their oil spill in the Gulf of Mexico, or Merck & Co and their trials with Vioxx, or GM and their 'Ignition Switch Recall'. Do **_not_** cut corners to try to save profits because the damage done and payouts you will have to make when those foundations fall will outweigh anything you made trying to pocket the initial difference.

Do things right the first time, because if you don't, you may not get the chance to do them right the second.

FINANCES AND ECONOMY

"Wealth consists not in having great possessions, but in having few wants."

– Epictetus

 $\mathcal{T}$ he issue of wealth in society is one so strong, whether in losing or gaining, that it simply cannot be ignored by any self-respecting individual. Whether you care for it or not, money is a massive part of day-to-day life and only by understanding and learning can we gain, lose, or disregard it all together.

To put it bluntly, most people are poor. Perhaps they are not starving or roofless, but very few people are capable of affording all of their wants and a good many cannot even afford a good portion of their needs. The problem is that no matter how prosperous society at large may become, someone is always going to have to clean the gutters, and assuming no radical shift in society takes place (and on most ends, even if it does) only those who cannot afford to say no will take the job; and there are far more dirty jobs that need doing than there will ever be not needed to be done.

Not that this is such a bad thing, mind you. While everyone should be able to afford needs, luxuries *should* be expensive and take work, since to afford said luxuries and status symbols is one of the greatest incentives someone could ever have; as it is one of the few pleasures that is both tangible and socially applicable (which is why reward-based systems are so efficient, if not easily corruptible). A stable society needs those who are willing to clean sewers and most people are too stubborn or flimsy to undertake such a burden completely of their own honourable merit.

But it is neither jobs nor people's willingness to take them that is the issue. Because we do not yet live in a post-scarcity society, *that* is what I will be addressing here; how to afford such needs before attaining your wants and the answer to that is very simple.

To save money. Sort of.

Now, I know you may very well be yelling *"But I can't save! All of my profits go to my bills and I still barely make ends meet!"* to which I reply: Why are you doing that? I cannot hear you.

Anyways.

Many people claim they do not make enough to put their money to better use, but more often than not, I see otherwise. They squander! Piece by piece it goes down the drain, so little and gradual that they barely notice.

It is the same principle as weight loss: the true villain is not the sweets, but the salad dressing. When people diet, they will count calories on their chicken, but not the breading. They will neglect to count the calories of the nuts they eat, reasoning that these calories are so small they needn't be added. They will drink coffee with cream, add sugar to cereal, mix sauces and gravies, eat crackers and chips, and all the while these little dents build up while the sufferer does not understand why they aren't losing as much weight as they should be. Because there is a stark difference between what they 'think' they're eating versus what they're actually eating. So too is it with finance.

Sometimes you'll finish a task and feel the need to treat yourself. Other times you will be stressed and relax with a luxury. I cannot even count how many times I've seen a man so concerned about bills and payment that he goes down to his local bar and drowns himself in expensive drinks.

I hate to break your spirit, but solving a problem does not mean you need a reward. Solving the problem *is* the reward as it means you no longer have to deal with the problem; anything extra is just a bonus, and that little bonus snowballs into big bonuses that go down the drain when they would have been put to better use going to something more needed. People will work so hard to save up money, then feel so good about saving that they feel they can afford to spend, and it is paradoxical to withstand the urge to treat yourself and then feel so good about your discipline and willpower that you buy yourself a treat.

All that being said, there is an equally serious problem I need to address, and that is the victimization of the poor for not depriving themselves of every worldly nicety until they become rich. *"You should not own a nice watch," "You could have bought cheaper shoes," "You should eat more rice and beans," "How can you be poor when you have a nice X?"* So on, so forth.

Do not mistake me, some of these criticisms *do* have merit. I have known poor people who were entirely at fault for the fact they were poor because they chose to go to concerts over paying rent, but these criticisms are often applied in the *wrong direction*. They are not applied to those who *insist* upon luxury, where they should be, but applied to those who have *any* luxury; as if man should be a termite automaton who works and sleeps and works and sleeps, eating only gruel and living as a Spartan until they make enough to earn a passive income.

I do not agree.

It is a harsh, cruel, and unfulfilling life to be made to work to enjoy the sparse free time you have. The people who make these criticisms will acknowledge the value of morale and happiness to good workmanship but will happily blind themselves where it comes to the personal lives of those same workers once they put up their work boots and settle down to relax at home; and they do this because the fact that there are many who live in a society where poverty is the norm is an uncomfortable prospect to tarry with.

People shouldn't have to sleep on the floor and endure the harsh cold and heat until they 'make it', they should be able to have the comforts that make life easier to get through regardless. It is okay for people to have nice things that make their lives enjoyable. It is okay that people use what money they have to add satisfaction and ease to their existence. That's what the money is *for*, in case you've forgotten. Instead, to reiterate, these criticisms ought to be levied against those who sacrifice fulfilling needs *for* luxuries, rather than people that have luxuries at all. It is unfortunate that life does not care what is fair, and that by necessity, many in the latter group could benefit from the advice for the former regardless, which is where we get to what to *do* with that money.

Most any mogul would tell you that when left to its own devices, money will make itself. Accrue interest. This is why some of the first things the soon-to-be-wealthy do when they get their paycheck is invest, they

Look at me.

Look me in wherever you imagine my eyes to be.

When I say *invest*, I do not mean: 'In Crypto-Currency' or 'In your car', or in anything with depreciating value ("Depreciating value" means: "To become less valuable over time/with use"). Investing is not like gambling, though there are risky investments. The layman's description of an investment is: 'You put up money. That money is then given to a business in the form of/part of a loan. You then receive interest based on the proportion of *your* money that made up that loan.' Simple.

Investments can be risky in that the business who takes out that loan *could* default on it and not be able to pay it back; such as if they go bankrupt or if the loan cannot be reasonably expected to be repaid due to miscalculations of potential profit (like a mine having less yield than originally thought). But you mustn't fret.

Not only are there often laws that protect investors who are frauded/lose money (in the form of receiving some of the insurance payout the business gets) but you can also often specify the kind of risk you w*ant* to take. You can choose to invest in low-risk businesses with a low chance of defaulting when you speak with an investment manager. You can also invest in multiple businesses, so even if one *happens* to default, you still have something to fall back on. You can even decide what happens to the money you *make* from these investments; whether they go directly into your bank account for you to spend spend or whether they're re-invested so you make more the next time.

Likewise you do not often require a vast amount of capital to begin. You do not need millions, since even multiple *smaller* piles can make up a vast hoard. In most circumstances, you'll only need about a pittance of your paycheck.

You can study the market and decide what businesses you'd like to invest in, if they are taking investments, or you can just ask an investment manager to do it, often at your local bank. They'll usually be more than happy to do so as part of the service of you banking with them.

Finally, certain laws *may* be different depending on your country/province/state/area. The next time you visit your bank, just ask and a meeting will likely be arranged where they'll take you through the whole process. It's really very simple, I promise, and your future self will thank you.

The point of all this is to get what is called 'Passive Income'. A passive income is, as it sounds, income you receive passively; without actually doing anything. There is this lovely quote from Warren Buffett (very rich man, which of course means he's qualified) that goes:

> *"If you don't find a way to make money while you sleep, you'll work until you die."*

The point of having investments, then, is to make money while you sleep. As a general rule of thumb, anything that will allow you to gain a passive income will serve you well and is worth most any amount of time and effort to set up properly.

. . .

This is why I recommend reducing this aforementioned squandering as much as able. The recommended way to do it is to set aside a portion of every paycheck, whether it be 10%, 20%, or 30%, and use it solely for investments. Passive income. Any 'treat' money can be used this way as well. This method is so prolific amongst the elites that many banks will even offer a service to *automatically* deduct any amount of money coming into your bank account *exclusively* to use it for your specified investments. The more you do this, the more money you make; and you will be shocked to see just how much you *don't* miss the money you put into it.

Much like how, in placing food in front of a person, whether they are hungry or not, they are likely to nibble; so too is it with money. If you *have* it, you are tempted to *spend* it. This is where the benefit of it not entering your hands to begin with comes in, where it can make money for you without you ever considering whether or not you should get a new paintjob.

Often, when people get the first, big paycheck, they tend to spend it on the fancy things they wanted rather than investing it further, or when white-collar workers with big bonuses buy new cars instead of putting it in a fund, or when you don't get a text back right away so you send that risky double-text and then a third and it really spirals out of control until you're constantly playing catch-up with trying to undo the damage of all the texts you keep sending until it keeps you up at night ten years later over how embarrassing that was when really they were just gonna block you regardless.

Look, the point is, you must always think long-term, lest decisions benefit you only in the short-term. Much like driving, try to have your eyes on where you want to be as much as is reasonable, and do all that you can to ignore what detours may limit you in getting there.

Now, as much as I think money is not required to live well, I'm not going to lay philosophical hooey on you in this chapter. Having your basic needs met is important, and upon that line I would implore you to do your own research and decide the best financial plan for yourself. If you cannot stick to it, arrange for it to be stuck to by forces outside of you. Just do not forget about the lessons you've learned; that sacrifices must be made for successes to be grasped later, and that the more you take out for yourself, the less you will have when you need it.

TO SERVE MAN

The capacity for kindness and compassion within man is as limitless as its cruelty; and throughout all of history there abounds stories of people risking everything, and often sacrificing it, to do what they believe is right in helping others. From those who hid Jews from the Nazis at great personal risk, to Muslims and Christians shielding eachother in prayer from would-be attackers.

The capacity for goodness and self-sacrifice is easily one of the greatest, most noble qualities of mankind.

It is a shame, then, that the most renowned proverb is about the road to hell being paved with good intentions. The difference between helping someone and hindering them has the same breadth of  distance as what we intend to do versus what we actually do, and often through no fault of our own. No man should be expected to possess divine wisdom, nor full lifetimes of experience, and yet it is through a lack of these that anyone can err in their judgements.

But there are ways we can do better...

.   .   .

There are two primary ways in which people fail at properly helping others. The first is that they draw upon their own experiences rather than the experience of the sufferer, falsely presuming that what helped them must also help others. This is the more reasonable of the two. Because we *only* have our own experiences to draw on, it makes sense that we'd use them as a springboard to give advice. In fact, most people already seem quite aware of this; often prefacing their advice with

"This is what worked for me..."

or some paraphrasing thereof, and it could be refined further by using your experiences as the *other person's* springboard. I.E:

"This helped me, because of [X] and [Y] reasons. Do you think it would help you?"

and going from there.

The second is far less reasonable. But luckily, much simpler. And it is when people presume that just because something is easy, it is helpful; and because it is hard, it is hindering. And I am not referring to basic encouragement for discipline or 'hard work' or any such thing. I mean it in a much simpler way; where people believe that by making something easier for another person, they are helping them, when in fact it is rarely so.

Humor me for a minute. Imagine the path of life as a type of obstacle course, and every person alive lining up to run it. Every runner, regardless of who they are, will face some obstacles.

Some will face their biggest obstacles far earlier than most, while for others it will start off easily and get harder as it goes along. Others still will have trouble, not for the number of obstacles, but for their own dexterity. The point being that we, from highest to low, all go through our own life-struggles; even when it may not seem so.

Humans are social animals. We tend to feel best and most fulfilled when we are with our trusted 'tribe' members. Achievements, food, rituals, fears, and all, they seem to feel even better when shared with others. This is an evolutionary trait, because when we were just cavemen living in... ah.... caves, it was extremely important that we work together to overcome the obstacles we faced. This is how we've made it so far as a society, and our teamwork is just as important now as it ever was. We work best *together*, it is hard written into our DNA to *help eachother* overcome the obstacles in this course, which is why it can be so awful when the assistance we offer serves only to weaken those we struggle to help.

We must always be mindful, for it is easy to become addicted to being helped back up once you fall. And when you find out how addicted you are, it is when you have forgotten how to stand. For others, the feeling of *helping* is addictive, because it means those around us have no choice but to cherish and yearn for us for reasons that don't depend upon pesky personality traits we're self-conscious over. For many, the feeling of social approbation and the affection of our peers is so addicting that to remain in dire circumstances, either to help or be helped, is preferable to recovering from them, for the sake of the sympathy and approval we receive.

Keep this in mind when I say that in running this obstacle course, we always have the option to help others. We can hold certain platforms up to help them run across, we can jam gears to keep them from being knocked off, we can throw ladders down to help ease the uphill climb. This is usually how it goes with children. We help them overcome the big problems while letting them handle the small ones, all in order to help them build up to handling the big problems on their own. It can work similarly for a friend or loved one, when they have gone through a few too many large obstacles, one after another, that we want to smooth some over to make it easier on them. That's often-what partnerships are all about to begin with.

But there comes a certain point where you are no longer allowing someone to run the obstacle course for themselves at all. Where they cannot overcome the large problems on their own and even the small ones must be smoothed over. Where you're just running it for them.

As we learn and grow, so do our skills, so too does our ability to problem-solve. To this end, every obstacle we face, even the ones we are assisted with, ought to teach us something, provide some experience. But what experience can it provide *us* when it is done **for** us? What can we teach others when we deny them the very experiences those lessons would have applied to?

This is why one of the first lessons we ought to impart upon our children is to 'try again', in an attempt to encourage them to figure things out for themselves. And it is only when they continue to struggle that we ought to provide some manner of guidance. If we assist them before they even have the chance, then they may grow dependent; whereas if we *never* assist them, they may grow despondent. But perhaps the greatest tragedy of rendering too much assistance at all is that *you* grow tired.

When you do so much, running the course for two, you are effectively halving your output. Not only are you not helping them in the way that matters, but you are also making yourself less able to manage your *own* obstacles, causing a feedback loop; and I've met far too many enablers to be amused with it. Because that's what it is, *enabling*; and *that's* why such a thing is so looked down upon, because not only does it weaken them, but also yourself.

These are the more socially apt examples. But there are morbid ones too; stories of divers and climbers trying to remove the bodies of their fallen comrades from deep sea caves and snowy-mountain peaks only to die in the attempt.

That's why they warn you that some caves are blocked off; because it's safer to avoid the bodies than trying to dislodge them. That's why Green Boots is still there and has been for nigh twenty years. Because, forgive my stone heart, it's better for only *one* person to fall behind.

· · ·

Even so, I'm not telling you that you shouldn't help people. On the contrary, I'm a big fan of avoiding pointless suffering, which is why I'm writing this essay to begin with. What I am trying to impart is that there is a very firm line between enabling weakness and helping overcome obstacles, a line which everyone must learn if they are to get the best out of their circumstances.

Are you preventing someone from facing obstacles because *you* believe they are not ready, regardless of what *they* say about it? Then you are constricting them. Are you pushing them to endure hardships even as they've repeatedly asked for help against largely unfair circumstances? Then you are abandoning them. Do you seem to help them with the same problems over and over as they keep coming back for you to solve them? Then you are enabling them. Have they shown no interest in either learning from or overcoming their obstacles and just opt to offload them onto you? Then you are babying them. So on, so forth.

The golden rule is that so long as they are actively trying to solve the problem, and are eager to learn, it is okay to assist them *provided* they ask for it. It's also fine to assist someone who's problem rests on a lack of expertise rather than a lack of wisdom; since no one can be an expert in all things and that's part of the benefit of banding together to begin with, so that each person can benefit from the support and expertise of another.

When it comes to emotional support, keeping hope alive is rarely ever a bad thing; and you must never forget to be able to entrust people with responsibility and hardships. Conversely, if you believe they are out of their depth, whether by a lack of expertise or wisdom both, that is no excuse to intervene. Simply offer your experience and assistance if they wish to take it, and if they refuse, allow them. People are much stronger, much more durable, than they might seem; but they will never know just how much if they are constantly being given ways to escape from the test. Even their own pride can be an obstacle that must be learned from; and if they refuse to learn and just keep stepping on the proverbial rake, well then... I already mentioned Green Boots, didn't I?

. . .

Also, I lied earlier. There is a much more sinister third way to fail at helping others; and it is where you only pretend at assisting them in order to fulfill ulterior goals.

Allow me an example:

Have you ever met a man who encouraged you to exercise, eat right, and wake up with the birds each morning so that you may have a body as fit and muscular as theirs? And when informed that you cannot follow such advice due to life circumstance, instead of altering the advice, they belittle you for not being like them? *"Not my fault your genetics suck* (unlike mine)," *"You're just too soft (unlike me)."*

Or perhaps you have met a woman who's comforting words seemed suspiciously like a misrepresentation? *"If your significant other isn't doing whatever you want, you should break up with them (and be single like me)," "If you're feeling bad, you should go on a lunch date with me (and pick up the tab)."*

Or perhaps a person whose tough love was more 'tough' than 'loving'? *"The only mental illness is a bad attitude (because I can blame you for that)," "Why are you upset? I was only joking. You need to calm down (and let me keep insulting you)".*

The reason they do this is because they don't actually want to help you. The road to hell may well be paved with good intentions, sure, but it can be paved with bad ones just the same.

What they're really doing is abusing the misfortunes of others in a round-about way to compliment themselves. If they believe that anyone can do as they do, and no one does, then they must be better than everyone, right? It's not that you have a broken leg, dummy, it's that you don't have the willpower they do. Or to put it another way: *They are superior for their willpower.* It's not that you have different standards of what's acceptable, it's that *they know their worth* whereas you do not. It's not that you go through different struggles, it's that *they are better for getting over theirs so simply*; and the greatest indicator for the fact that these people feel this way is that they tend to get very *antsy* when someone approaches their level. If someone is tougher, they must not be a 'real man' in other respects. If someone is comfortable in their introspection, they must be a 'sour puss'. If someone stands up for themselves, they must not be able to 'take a joke'.

The common pattern here is that once you begin to match up with their standards, or apply their own back at them, these standards will always conveniently shift in just such a way to maintain their superiority. They will suddenly remember details that make their accomplishments slightly more legitimate when you bother to match it. The suffering they have undergone will, by sheer coincidence, require far more than the canned wisdom that they offer *your* suffering. When someone comes along who matches their traits and output, some arbitrary metric that applies only to themselves will be invented as an explanation for why it's okay for them and not others.

These people do not want to help you. They want to *look good*, and your problems are the canvas for which they present it.

Accomplishments really are the narcissist's worst nightmare, because they have to make everything seem so easy for them whilst also making it hard enough to be worth bragging about, like my friend Davey who always told me to not make excuses in Basketball until, when I had been practicing and could totally whoop his ass, suddenly claimed he couldn't face off against me anymore since the "accident" caused him to go "blind". Whatever that means.

Anyways, all that being said, be mindful not to confuse *insensitive* advice with *malicious* advice. Someone may well say that you are too emotional and need to be more stoic because they don't want you to react when they cross your boundaries, true. Or perhaps they really do think you're too sensitive and should be more tolerant of stressors and just communicate it poorly. Not everyone is a savant of rhetoric;

and people tend to talk how they listen. The best way to tell the difference is to try to discern *why* they believe this advice will help you. If you inquire, and they give you a legitimate, though perhaps clumsy, justification, you may see fit to try it out. If their justification is based on leaps of logic and hair-thin reasonings that they try to reach to connect to your problems, they may well be trying to hide their true motives, even from themselves.

Past behaviour is also an excellent indicator. People who have actively demonstrated a kind and well-meaning motive behind their actions are much more likely to be trustworthy than people who have demonstrated a self-centered and hostile mindset. Same goes for those you are helping. Those who have demonstrated earnest attempts to overcome their problems are the most deserving of assistance when they fall short, and those who continue to try to pawn their struggles off onto others should be ignored until they have no choice but to try to do it themselves.

It is easy to tell, by sheer intuition if you apply it, the goals and motivations behind people's actions from how they speak to you. There are those in this world who will want you to grow from every encounter, every conversation, who's nigh every word overflows with respect to your potential and what will help you achieve it. And there are others who fear this. Those who's subtle jabs and pushes are always geared toward serving themselves, even at cost to you. These people do not respect you. They do not care about you the way you deserve to be cared about. Reach out with your instincts and realize this.

Neither you, nor I, nor anyone can save people from their own lives. As often as we might wish otherwise. Sometimes the only person who can save someone, especially from their own bad decisions, is themselves. To continue to jump in, to continue to play the role of Knight in Shining Armor is not to save a damsel or slay a dragon, but to deprive them of the chance to slay their own dragons, to rescue their own damn selves. The worst thing you

can do for these kinds of people is steal their problems out from under them.

If you want to help them, really really help them, then offer your compassion and emotional support for their lows, and your praise and respect for their highs; recognize them so that the struggles they undergo are not gone through in vain, and I promise that when they are ready, they will come to you for help if they really need it. And if they solve it all on their own, then all the better; for there is no greater struggle in life than our own inner turmoil. And there is no greater victory than to overcome it.

A SECRET WORTH KEEPING

"Man is not what he thinks he is, he is what he hides."
- André Malraux

Secrets are a constant of life. From when the first living thing was made until the last living thing dies, a secret will be kept from something, somewhere. This in itself is not concerning, nor should it be. Each person is entitled to their privacy and their own judgement as to what should and should not be revealed. The thing to focus on, then, is the motive as to *why*.

Secrets carry a bad rap. Despite being inherently neutral, much like propaganda, they have a particularly negative connotation. Perhaps understandably so. Our psyches tend to balk at being left in the dark at anything we'd consider concerns us and our affairs, but even a Christmas Present is a secret until it's reveled. In some cases, they can symbolize something far more cunning; secret influence, knowledge, hidden powers and blackmail, grand mysteries man was not meant to know. That sort of thing.

They have an almost addictive quality to them. Once something is labelled as a secret, regardless of what it is, there's almost a magical lure to try to unearth it; even to the point of obsession and self destruction (as anyone familiar with Mr. Eaten can tell you). They have a binding quality to them, where a grave secret shared can almost act as a fervent oath; tying two parties together until death, and even more light-hearted ones, no matter how small and gossip-filled they may be, can still be a delicious treat when shared amongst trusted peers.

...But why?

There is something fulfilling about being 'in' on the 'in-joke'. Being able to tell those kinds of funny jokes and stories that only you and a select group of people know is not just socially beneficial, but psychologically so. You are a "member" of this group. You are welcome here. You have history here.

This same sense of belonging is perverted by hazing rituals, where one must be humiliated, harmed, or harm another to be welcome. You belong in this group, yes... but you're also at the bottom of the totem pole. You are welcome. But barely. And you must keep seeking the approval of the more senior members, affirming their own place in the hierarchy and never nay-saying against the status quo.

These are the same types of tactics a lot of social groups use, the same types of tactics a lot of *cults* use. Cults who, ironically, often form their existence around the uncovering or protecting of a secret. In this perversion, you are only welcome so long as you affirm the social order. If you disagree with it, you may lose your rank. If you lose your rank, you may be exiled. No longer welcome. Rejected.

. . .

In evolutionary psychology, your brain uses chemical rewards to encourage good behaviour. That's why eating feels good, working out feels good, sleeping feels good. A lot of marketing and chemical research abuses these reward centers, trying to get us to associate the good feeling with their product. This is even how addictions can be caused; but for the most part it never really lasts. Mostly.

Because your reward centers have 'caps' to them; where something will eventually *stop* feeling good, and maybe even make you feel worse. That's why rest and masturbation have diminishing returns of pleasure, there *is* 'too much of a good thing' and if you do it too much, it can hurt you. So your brain has built-in limiters to prevent you from being encouraged to go too far. Mostly.

Because there is a form of pleasure that does *not* have a cap. It can increase exponentially, never diminishing in chemical love. And that is social approbation. The acceptance and love of the group.

In nearly every context of human history there was no way you could be *too* loved. The tribe was protection, it was food, it was safety, it was comfort, you required the tribe to satisfy all needs; spiritual, biological, and psychological. The *more* beloved you were, the more of each of these you would receive. And the more loved you *weren't*, the more likely you were to face exile. Death. There was rarely a condition where it was 'bad' to be wanted.

And then social media was invented and messed everything up. That's a story for a different time though.

The point is that this is the reason you see people do insane stunts to get attention or to be welcome in a certain clique. This is why some people rate situations involving social humiliation as more frightening than bodily harm. This is why the bad memories of messing up social situations are among some of the most traumatic. Because in our only slightly more evolved cave-man brains: these things mean we *die*, and *worse* than die, because at least if we died beloved then our family and friends will be cared for after we pass on. If we are hated? Rejected? *Nothing* is saved.

. . .

Perhaps this is where the strength of the secret lies. Not only in the superiority of knowing what others do not, not only in the pragmatic gains of power and influence it unfolds before you, but that whether it be good or ill, the idea of *knowing*, that sense of being irrevocably tied to the in-group, means you can *never* be rejected.

Here, among the great expanse of the world, the cosmos, of life itself; to *know* what others should not means you are chosen. You are welcome here.

Perhaps this is why people hide secrets too. Much like a product can be more or less valuable based purely on its scale of circulation, so too can information. To know things others do not is a virtue; and it is even why some mentors and teachers will intentionally lead their apprentices astray so their own place in the hierarchy remains unchallenged. Their knowledge purely to themselves.

There is also the secondary reason people hide secrets; the threat of social ostracism. To do something shameful, and then hide it so you remain unjudged over it. To feel the secret, shared to no one, gnaw away at you. Who else can you tell? And you do *want* to tell, don't you? Because a secret shared by two is belonging. What is a secret only you know, then? Something you've seen or done that's so forbidden that anyone else knowing would not connect you to them but sever them from you. Where do you belong now?

As punishing and contradictory as it can be, curiosity and the desire to know is a good thing. It shows a lot about one's character and it's certainly not a trait that one should deem punishable.

The reason why impersonal knowledge may be kept in the dark is mostly out of concern. This is apparent in many forms of literature and media where in countless stories the antagonist is able to terrorize and grow more powerful because of the evil or twisted secrets they may have uncovered, information that should have been kept better hidden and should remain hidden so it corrupts no other... yet... *does* information corrupt you? On the contrary, it seems it would purify you. It allows you to see new horizons and grasp more opportunities than you could before. And yet the obsession that can come from such questions... The distance one would go... It is a uniquely harmful thing.

For the sayings that "knowledge is power" and "power corrupts" both exist, and together lead to some unfortunate conclusions.

Information is a neutral party in all this. No thing can be 'evil' just because there are those who use it to nefarious ends; and while it may be harmful, so too can most anything can be used toward malevolent purposes regardless of what it is. That is still no reason to lock everything away. While it is true that some things are more naturally inclined toward malevolence than not, a thing or concept in itself cannot be wicked; that trait only depends upon the person who uses it.

This is especially relevant for taboos, where many parents do not want to teach their children about such things because they want to maintain their innocence, but they do it in the wrong way. Your charge is not going to remain innocent forever and by depriving them of information you are only making it harder for them to grow and become independent. You might think that your child is simply not mature enough to handle such subjects, but by withholding certain information, the only thing you are really changing is the pain they go through while learning about it, and from whom they learn it from.

As much as we might wish otherwise, not talking about things does not make them go away. People will still be curious and still want to know, *especially* over the concept of generational trauma. What's the alternative? That they go through their lives *knowing* something is wrong but never knowing what or why? That is not the fate we ought to wish on loved ones. Especially since it can easily get worse, causing them to go to the wrong people who give bad advice and bad perspectives on what is wrong rather than to those who know the truth and will let them decide how to react for themselves.

And just to be clear I'm not saying there *shouldn't* be any taboos, there are certainly parts of life that should be kept personal and between close bonds rather than spread about, but what I am saying is that just because something should be kept quiet doesn't mean it shouldn't be *talked about*.

If secrets really do have the bonding power they seem to, then let us use them to get closer rather than push everyone away.

DEATH AND LOSS

"Death is nothing to us, since when we are, death has not come, and when death has come, we are not."
– *Epicurus*

---

*I*t is difficult to know what to do when someone dies. What to say. What clothes to wear. Where to stand when the eulogy is being given. What to do after it is over. It is so difficult to do any of these things that it can be hard to compartmentalize, at the time, that you're never going to see this person again.

You'd think that would be the point of the funeral rites to begin with, but it doesn't seem so. It is difficult to know what an appropriate grieving process even is, at times.

When someone dies, what we most often mourn is not the life itself that is lost, but the potential that went with it. We do not mourn so deeply for the elderly, for they have already lived such a full life; seen so much, done so much, imparted so much. But what of the young? A partner? A child? How much could they have done if only life were kinder?

We mourn the hours we could have shared. But it seems strange to mourn what might have been, like a boy crying at an ice-cream he could have had. Crying for all the moments we could have had. They could have had. The tender smiles and warm comforts of their domestic life. All whilst appreciating the moments we *did* share. Even former anxieties and scrapes can turn to playful memories. A nostalgia for what used to torment us. A resolution that it was a life worth living, time worth having, and yet a cry that there couldn't have been more.

Perhaps that is why it can be so *difficult* to mourn. Why our feelings, from longing to numbness, to nostalgia and anger, can be so difficult to parse. Because there is at once both an acceptance and a rejection of death. An: *"It must happen."* And: *"It should not have."*

I remember, when I was young, seeing books like 'The Fall of Freddie the Leaf' and 'Big Cat, Little Cat' on my mother's shelf. Books she read after the death of my sister; and I read them too and I did not understand them. Because I did not know how loss stays with us.

There are things we do not lament in the same way. Most do not grieve for a pet, or an item, or an insect the same way they do for a person because there is an aspect of self-expression and will that come with the individual. And we do not grieve for a stranger because we do not know *how* to grieve for them. Is it inappropriate to weep for someone as if they had an affect on your life? Is it inappropriate to convince yourself you could have known them when there is no way to be sure?

All we are able to lose are those close to us. By their very nature, the losses we feel are the hardest we could have felt.

And then there are some who feel as if they did not grieve properly at all. As if they didn't cry hard enough, feel enough, suffer enough at this passing; the guilt that comes with not honouring loss as it should be honoured. Yet they do accept it. They accept that something has come and gone. They accept that a life has been lived, even for a short time, and then was not. They accept and carry on. As we all must.

Loss is a natural part of life and something that every person can feel. There is no wrong way to accept loss. Only we know how those closest to us should be honoured, how they would have wanted to be honoured, in our own hearts and minds.

For as much as we may try to prevent it, and take extra pains to avoid it, loss remains unavoidable. So prolific, so much the cause of such endless suffering that hundreds of religions have devoted much of their faith to entrusting that all that is lost will one day be regained, somewhere, sometime. And philosophies likewise sprung up, whether to explain how to prevent this suffering, or why it was okay to lose, or even why it was good.

They say: "Death is necessary so we appreciate the time we have," or "Death is good because without it, we wouldn't know how to live," or "Death teaches us to value those close to us," and yet these are just balms to soothe the wound in our hearts. Ones that feel like they will never close. Because loss doesn't just affect the dying, it effects those who must live on after. The constant questions of the things unsaid, unfinished, the roads never taken.

But the things you said, what you shared, the paths you did walk are still there.

Would choosing another path have made the loss easier to bare? Would that really have been the difference that gives you the strength to carry on?

I think you've done fine so far.

I think you'll be okay.

If it truly concerns you that much that you might lose something before expressing how you really feel, then it is up to you to make it known. Tell your loved ones how you feel, let your employer know your intentions, let your leader see who they are leading, write about your thoughts and motivations to the paths you've seen and hewed for yourself and never ever forget that while something close to you may be lost, something so dear that you feel you will never be whole again, that YOU are still here.

When I left my homeland, I had to leave behind everything I had ever known. The hot summers and bitter winters, the people I waved to, the layout I knew like the back of my hand. My family. My past. Even my best friends.

We were friends since the earliest days in highschool. We did everything together. I went to some of their weddings! I drank wine up my ass with their help! We played hookie and skipped school and galivanted across town. We would go to eachother's houses in the pitch dark of night to rattle on their windows and wake eachother, sneaking out to run, hooting and hollering, up and down the streets. We played jokes, shared secrets, and bled time and again as the price for eachother's antics.

I loved them with a love that would make Spartan poets weep.

I still do.

But in leaving my home, I had to leave them behind too. And in pursuing my own ambitions, and they theirs, life problems would get in the way; other obligations would take us from what sparse games we could share and when I lost much of the social media that kept me in touch to begin with, it seemed like the final straw.

I haven't spoken to some of them in years.

The last I heard, the group just fell apart. It is not there anymore.

And it gives me a misery in my heart like nothing else. Like the journey of Odysseus, to go so far to come home only to find that the home he returned to had changed in his absence. What he felt was his home no longer existed.

Just like mine doesn't.

The poem 'Around the Corner' by Charles Hanson Towne strikes a sickening chord.

I remember trees from my childhood that are no longer there.

I remember paths I have walked that no longer exist due to erosion.

I remember my elementary school that has closed down.

And like Odysseus, I just want to lay down and cry. To sink into the Earth.

But...

I still laugh at the antics of my friends, when I think of those fond memories we made together.

I still feel comfort from the memory of resting in the shade of a tree that is no longer there.

I still feel the warmth of nostalgia in imagining myself walking down my block, so changed, as I have changed.

If I want to live forever, if I must live forever, this is something that's bound to happen.

Eventually I will lose everything.

But I will also gain things anew.

I will make new friends, new memories, things so bright and vivid they bring tears to the eye.

And I will hold them just as close as I hold the experiences I have already had.

For these too make up who I am.

Who we are.

. . .

The silver lining of loss is that, in a roundabout way, you never actually lose these things either.

The things that are lost are still there, in me. In my memories, the way I move, the way I talk, the way I breathe.

The tree may not exist, the streets may have changed, the spaces I spent my time running through the halls may not be present, but they are still there in me.

The fact that I can no longer draw on them in the waking world means little in comparison to what we shared before.

They will always be there. Always exist.

And will, for as long as we hold them close.

CONFIDENCE AND SELF-ESTEEM

"No one can make you feel inferior without your consent."
- Eleanor Roosevelt

---

*T*he problem with having low self-esteem is squarely in the fact that it compounds every other negative aspect; including how difficult it can be to gain positive self-esteem at all. Much like with depression, when you are in that stoop of despair, it can be difficult to even find reason to bring yourself out of it. But we can at least define the two main areas from which confidence arises:

The first, from internal sources. These can be a sense of accomplishment and duty, pride from deeds; a sense of steadfastness and authenticity, pride from character; or from a sense of expertise and ability, pride from superiority.

And the second from external sources. This can be confidence gained from the support of others, the trust from our mentors, the respect of our underlings, and the approval of our loved ones.

. . .

Let me be clear and say that, though there is often a stigma against it, there is nothing *wrong* with a sense of pride gained from the respect and love of those around us. We are social animals; we are designed by our very nature to yearn for the support of our tribe. To not have this kind of approval and encouragement, *especially* during our formative years, can be destructive to our psyche. Our sense of values is often first formed by our family, and then later synthesized with those of our friends and acquaintances. Every piece of evidence I have ever seen comes to the same conclusion: that when people lack the sense of safety and belonging they need when growing up, they will not be well-adjusted adults, for one reason or another.

There is nothing wrong with wanting to know that people support and believe in you. The lone wolf archetype may seem cool from an individualist perspective, but in the wild, the lone wolf dies cold and hungry; for they too are pack animals. It is admirable that one attempts to achieve on their own but remember that doing so at the cost of cooperation only ensures you'll be the best player on the losing team. Independence should always be respected, but teamwork should always be encouraged.

What people *mean* to advise against is depending *too much* on the approval of others. We must seek our *own* approval first and foremost. To be happy and satisfied with who we are will always be better than the tribe being happy with us at the cost of hating ourselves.

It is these two factors combined that come to form a healthy sense of confidence and self-esteem. If it is the second that is lacking, then it is an easy enough fix. With that sense of trust and belonging our tribe places in us, so too will our confidence begin to knit itself together. You can even watch this happen in real time, when someone first joins a community, unsure and insecure, and slowly, with the encouragement of others in it, become a more assertive and self-assured person.

This is also what makes it so easy to abuse. If this individual happens to fall into the wrong crowd, and they learn through example and repetition that the way to gain approval is to perform unhealthy and self-destructive acts, then they are doomed to be broken apart; either by a final collapse into acts so terrible that even their own sense of self will not abide by it, or in being ripped away from the only sense of belonging they have and be forced to start over from scratch. It is vital that people learn, from the example of those most immediately around them, what healthy relationships and support systems look like, whether this be parent-to-child, teacher-to-student, or even fictional settings with characters forming a bond in a healthy and mutually supportive way. None of these are shameful, and all of them are preferred over the alternatives.

. . .

On the other hand, if it is the first aspect that is lacking, that of internal respect, the issue becomes a bit more difficult. If someone feels too poorly about themselves, even much of the best outside encouragement can be wasted since the afflicted will not be able to believe it anyways. It is difficult because their confidence *must* come from within. But, thankfully, is also more secure in doing so.

When it is our view of ourselves that is lacking, often based on one of the three archetypes, it is then in *pursuit* of these archetypes that changes it. Easier said than done, for our lack of self-esteem makes it difficult to pursue much of anything.

I remember coming to this realisation some time ago. In part with working alongside others who suffered from a distinct mix of go-getter attitude and shot self-esteem, and in part due to my own turmoil with my idea of who I *ought* to be not matching with how I was acting.

I knew that if I kept putting things off, kept delaying the process, my potential was infinite. So long as possibilities were endless, so too were my relative capabilities and powers. It wasn't 'my' fault these traits were found lacking, it was the environment I was in! And my complete obstinance to changing anything *about* my environment had nothing to do with it!

But in truth, it was like this because I was afraid of the possibility that I would try and fail anyways. Because so long as I never tried, so long as I never *really* applied myself, I could always rationalize that I would be superior if only I did. But if I *did* apply myself. If I really did give it all I had and *still* failed... Where would I be then? *What* would I be then?

And this mindset persisted until I watched a certain episode of Avatar: The Last Airbender, wherein a protégé is anguished over his inability to unlock a certain power, and his mentor remarks that it is because he feels too much shame. The protégé rebukes him, telling them that he feels *pride*! That's he's never *been* more proud! And his mentor gently corrects him:

"Pride is not the opposite of shame, but its source. True humility is the only antidote to shame."

I realized that I was not afraid of failing *itself* but instead of the shame and judgement of *others* seeing me fail; and my defense was to turtle into myself and never attempt anything so nobody could use it to attack me. But what were their opinions worth to me? Why was I so *willing* to take the insults of people I never cared about to heart?

I had to come to terms with the fact that if I never accepted a willingness to fail, I would never start anything. And I changed my outlook. Instead of practicing to avoid failure, I decided I was *okay* with failing, and began to practice.

And before I knew it, I actually got somewhere.

Yes, there were some people who saw my failings and had quite a laugh out of them, and yes, sometimes it still hurt. But because I was *okay* with feeling hurt, I was okay with continuing on *beyond* it. We must be okay with losing before we can win. It is because we are *not* okay with our cringe-ass selves that we cringe at all.

Of course there are some who feel differently, that it is their own view of themselves that is most important, and for them even little comforts like how nobody remembers the time we were total losers doesn't do much to help since *we* remember. And thus, it is *us* who must be okay with being who we are. It is us who must be okay with being human. With our idea of who we must be not lining up with who we are in the present. We hold ourselves to a standard fit for the future, as if our present self *should* simply be superior instead of working to *be* so. But it is the efforts that make it.

If we hold the measure of superiority between how well we can demean others, or how well they can demean us; it will make every aspect of life a competition; a terror. But to hold that the measure of superiority is doing better, being better, choosing better in similar circumstances than the ones we faced in days gone by, then we will find a satisfaction unlike any other.

It is the repeated failures, the lessons, the adjustments, the learning, the innovations, and the try-try-again that leads to success.

This is why, whatever your source of internal pride may be, the best method of gaining it is to simply *practice* it. Be it cooking, singing, reading the books you say you want to read, working out to get the body you say you want to have, making more friends and talking to people with the intention of learning something, defining for yourself what you believe is wrong and right based on your own views, or beginning to do what you *say* you are going to do; and if you don't know if you'll be *able* to, then say so before trying anyways to the best of your ability.

You will notice that a big theme of internal self-confidence is aligning who we are with who we want to be; making the attempt to bridge the gap. Likewise, external self-confidence comes with aligning people's perceptions of us with how we wish to be perceived.

Take note of both, for there are few ways to lose respect in either case faster than proving yourself unreliable (whether as major as making promises and not following through, or as minor as being late to an arranged meeting), and being prone to excuses (the constant attempt to shift guilt away from yourself, as opposed to an *explanation*, wherein reasons for failure fell outside of your control. It is not your fault the store closed early when they said they were still open. It *is* your fault you slept in).

It is simply easier to respect yourself when you are someone worth respecting. It is no wonder people can be so lacking in self esteem when they carry so many qualities they find unsavoury. Self-doubt, cowardice, and a lack of willpower would make anyone feel as if they are not worth respecting, and in feeling so, it will become monumentally more difficult to embody the qualities you feel are worth it. But you must try. Little by little.

. . .

But there is another way our confidence can suffer, and that is when we are damaged by trauma. Some guilt we hold onto, or something done that makes us value ourselves less.

Many, after a terrible experience, will try to recover by over-correcting, as seen with any common phobia. One who is terrified of the outdoors will crowd themselves inside just as one who is terrified of the dark will keep their house grossly illuminated; but these things do not provide the control we long for over the situations that terrify us; they merely act as an unhealthy counterbalance.

If something happened to you, the best thing you can do for yourself and others in your life is to simply account for it. To see every person as a threat or every insult as a wound will not help you. Even attempting to surround yourself with that which makes you feel strong can be a slippery slope to unhealthy coping mechanisms. If you are constantly reactive for the traumas of the past, they will always be in your way.

You should chase your goals and live your life because you want to, of your own volition. Not out of some kind of reaction to a perception of how you ought to be or what might have happened to you. "*I should do this to get over the bad thing,*" is unhealthy, even if it seems reasonable. It is unhealthy because you are placed in mindsets where you are always haunted by what has passed. Instead, it ought to be shifted, more forward, more kind.

"I should do this because I believe I should do it, because it is what I want to do."

Your worth as a person does not lie in what *happened*, it is in who you **are**. The ways in which you heal must follow this paradigm. Is being reactive, being hostile or demure, is that who you imagined yourself to be? Is that worthy of you? If not, how is acting in such a way going to help you?

Do not surround yourself with things that remind you of what has happened. Instead, surround yourself with things that affirm your strength. These could be items, people, ideas, anything that gives you inspiration for a new plateau or goal, and helps you keep perspective.

But in all of this, the greatest way to earn universal respect is to treat yourself with dignity. It is not forceful, as rank cannot demand to be recognized, and he who holds it is the more pathetic for acting as if it can. It is not symbolic, for people to misconstrue and misunderstand. It is not actionable, as people disagree about which actions themselves are respectable to begin with.

Rather, it is a simple, gentle reminder that you are human and deserve to be treated as such. It is making deliberate, conscious choices for the betterment of yourself and those around you. It is seeing value in the time you have. It is a certainty that you and your ideals are worth protecting. That you are deserving of what you earn.

So treat yourself well, for your own sake.

ON THE NATURE OF WISDOM

"Any fool can know. The point is to understand."
- Albert Einstein

---

*I*t has been said that one of humanity's greatest advantages is the ability to teach others. To have compounding knowledge. So that fifty years of study and practice could be condensed into a single one for the next generation, only for them too to spend the next fifty practicing and studying to refine the next, all the way downward.

It is why, when looking back over a long scale of time, the average person living in a developed country today has a better quality of life than a noble did five hundred years ago. Better food, better medical care, better luxuries, you name it; and it is all thanks to our ability to add on to eachother's knowledge. To teach others as we have been taught, so that nobody has to start from square one.

. . .

But this only seems true on a generational scale. As far as we individuals go, it seems all too often that no matter what we do, our failures come back to haunt us constantly, putting us into a continuous loop of action and reaction because we try the same thing again and again in the hopes that it will turn out differently. But luckily this problem is solved almost as easily as any other, because it is not what you see that is wrong, but how you see it.

The paradox of wisdom is that one requires wisdom to begin with in order to see the value in it. If you were to encourage someone to study, say, philosophy, because you feel it would improve their outlook and perspective, it comes with the necessary caveat that they would have to see value in that change of outlook and perspective to begin with.

People's own perceptions of what makes up success often blinds them to the whole of what it takes to get there. I.E: If someone doesn't respect creativity, or charisma, it is very easy to attribute neither to someone's success; and even worse, to see these things as attributing to success, but only in the barest notion; missing all nuance that may go into such planning or articulation.

Therefore, to properly encourage change, one must start by instilling a sense of value within the qualities pursued.

Or, as Terry Pratchett put it:

"Calling its name, cursing and eventually pleading, the farmer wandered about looking for the crevasse in which his sheep was stuck. One might wonder why, having one hundred sheep, he would spend all day searching for one foolish beast, without realizing that perhaps the reason he has one hundred sheep is that he would spend all day searching for one."

The first thing that must be realized is that everyone learns differently just the same as we all have different talents and excel in different fields. Everyone is unique in what they enjoy learning about and how they process that information, even you, and you're going to be spending a lot of time with yourself so I suggest you learn your own best way rather quickly lest you suffer a lot of avoidable frustration.

I remember watching this movie a long time ago. I cannot remember what the movie was called, or what it was even about; I only remember that I was probably too young to have been watching it and that it had this subplot about a nerd teaching a jock about physics. I think. Anyways, the jock fails at every course that tried to prep him for this upcoming exam until the nerd begins rephrasing the questions in ways that align with the jock's sporty interests; at which point he understands them perfectly. The jock remarks about how easy this is, and the nerd teases him that you could teach a monkey about physics if you just rephrased the lessons in the context of bananas.

And whether or not this is true about monkeys, it is certainly true about people.

This is why you find so many pieces of media; lessons, essays, courses, even this book, trying to explain age old concepts in slightly different ways instead of just one singular source everyone cites; and it's because different people learn different things in different ways. An explanation that might make sense to you may be lost to another, and vice versa.

That's the thing about life. Despite how crazy and chaotic it may seem at times, there is usually a very precise way of going about things and doing them correctly and no matter how stubborn you are or how tough you might be, the universe is infinitely tougher and will not change eons of... whatever the hell it's up to in order to suit your individual needs. It is *you* who must change and adapt; as Charles Darwin himself came to the same conclusion: that it is not the fastest nor the strongest nor the smartest animal, but that which is the most adaptable that survives all challenges. It is what Taoists have known for thousands of years. That it is the tall, rigid, grand oak that gets washed away in the flood waters while the flexible bamboo remains where it is rooted.

In this, whether academically or philosophically, the universe is teaching you what it's been teaching everything since the beginning of time, and that is to adapt and change accordingly.

To *learn*.

And the lesson, no matter how punishing, will continue until you learn from it.

There is an idea that has been knocking around in my head for a while that I lovingly refer to as: "The Proliferation of Successful Strategies."

The idea is right as it says on the tin.

Suppose you come up against a brick wall. You want to go through. You try punching it, it doesn't work. You try climbing it, it doesn't work. You try tunneling under, it doesn't work. You go *around* it. It works. You carry on.

You encounter *another* brick wall. But it's different this time *because* you faced this obstacle before. Now instead of trial and error, the *first* thing you do is try going around it. And so long as it keeps working, you will not do anything else. Why would you?

This is the axiom of the proliferation of successful strategies. When something works, you do it again. This is the premise for evolution (genes get passed on to offspring, those carrying winning genes live long enough to reproduce, continuing the cycle. Those carrying losing genes fail. These genes are not caried over), and the premise for business management (businesses compete. Those with a winning strategy are not only able to cover expenses, but also expand. Those with a losing strategy dissolve), and even the premise for your own choices. The solutions you tend to gravitate toward in any given circumstance; for it is a nigh guarantee that whether you approach problems aggressively, cautiously, defensively, or even in some nuanced degree, the *reason* you do so is because it's *what worked before.*

This proliferation has an incredible advantage in that it consistently rewards maximum gains with minimal effort. Just as plants spread their veins through the softest of topsoil and the lion chases the slowest gazelle, so too do you exert the least amount of energy to gain consistent results. You do it because it works. You do not change strategy because this one has proven to work. You need expend no further brainpower, energy, effort, anything more than you're already familiar with in order to get the results you desire. Simple.

This proliferation also has an incredible disadvantage in that it actively *discourages* you from trying anything else. For all you know, you could have trained your legs until you could jump clean over this wall; and if you could, you could have saved an innumerable amount of time and energy spent walking around it. A superior strategy that was not pursued because gains would have been delayed and you have no reason to try it because you already have a winning strategy. You do not pursue new strategies because you know what *already works,* and so trying to do anything else is just a gamble on wasting more brainpower and energy in the attempt for, more often than not, no net gain.

If you have ever been in a position where you already knew what strings to pull to get the outcome you wanted, then you have witnessed proof of the advantage of this proliferation.

If you have ever been in a position where something you've done the same way for a long time was shaken up by seeing a way it could have been done easier, you have witnessed proof of the disadvantage of this proliferation.

Even further, there are no events where this is not true. Organisms that do not possess successful strategies do not continue to live. If you look onto slums and see the drugged and the homeless and the bedraggled and the petulant and think this may not be so, I implore you to think again; because the goal *you* believe they have is not the goal may *actually* have. For whatever they are, whoever they are, however they are, these are the strategies that have worked for them in the past to get what they wanted.

In areas of seeming madness, where someone acts contrary to their stated motivations, it is not necessarily the strategy that is flawed, but rather, the disconnect between what they are *consciously* trying to achieve against what they are *subconsciously* trying to achieve. They might believe they are formulating strategies to pursue their stated goal, when all their subconscious is doing is causing them to sabotage themselves in favour of a hidden one. The repeated attempts and repeated failures are a result of this disconnect.

So too can you see the true nature of others in this light. Whatever they tell you, what are their strategies geared to attain? What is their wisdom focused towards?

And the inverse is true too. People change when the strategies that were previously successful no longer yield the results they want. A pet will bark or meow to get your attention for dinner until you stop paying attention, whereupon they will scratch and bite at the couch. The toddler will throw a fit to get what they want for as long as it continues to *get* them what they want. People will invent new technologies in proportion to the obstacles ahead of them. Reward the strategies you want to see. Punish the ones you do not. And this goes for yourself most of all. Hold yourself accountable. Go the extra mile and explore new possibilities. Limitation is the mother of innovation.

By not heeding the lessons you see around you and interpreting them to help you grow wise, you will simply never grow. Unsuccessful strategies do not proliferate. Wisdom without substance is no wisdom at all. Take heed that I am not telling you that persistence does not grant favour. On the contrary, persistence and stubbornness are what yield more rewards than anything, it's just a matter of where you are to apply it that most people have trouble with. They do not learn, because the gate they are trying to open is *not the gate they are trying to open*. You could become the wisest in the world in the ways of staying in bed all day, but if that's not what you want, then how does it help you? It is not about learning much but understanding much, it is not about working hard but working intelligently, it is not about how much you can do but how you do it.

So go out there, observe the world around you, talk to people and listen to them, find what they learned, the methods your superiors used, and adapt as your ancestors did every day in order to not only live, but thrive in their environment. Who knows? You might actually learn something.

APOCALYPSE NOW-ISH

$\mathcal{J}$ fear for the future, just as much as I fear the future itself.

It's not any specific event I fear, rather, it's just the inevitable march of obsolescence. My greatest worry in regard to rampant technological progress isn't necessarily anything that has to do with the machine itself, or even A.I monsters, but just the slaying of the human spirit.

Elon Musk, who was called a flagship innovator of technology before the internet collectively decided to hate him, has noted that humans either must adapt alongside machinery, becoming cyborgs of a sort, or perish into oblivion, being able to do absolutely nothing better than a machine can.

Level with me for a minute.

The trend of working has always been around. Ever since we were early humans, every single member of society was needed to contribute. The whole point of children being treated as fully grown adults at twelve and the trend of chucking malformed babies off of cliffs was needed because the difference of a single person sucking up resources whilst being unable to work could be the difference between the tribe thriving and the tribe dying out. Every single hand, mind, and body was needed in order to reach maximum efficiency.

But because of the occasional surplus, things changed. Whenever there was TOO much food, people were able to sit around and think, and in sitting around and thinking, they came up with more efficient ways to do things: Toolmaking. As time went on and more and more tools being made meant that working became easier and easier, this rapid trend ensured that the 1700's where nigh every person worked in agriculture was already destined to be eclipsed by the modern day, where almost nobody does.

"Awesome," you might think, and I agree, it *is* quite awesome and not just because there are less farmers. It is awesome because with the freedom to work as you choose, people are more able to go into endeavours where they are really passionate. Where they receive fulfillment.

Granted, the same thing as happened with farming is already happening almost everywhere else too. You go into making cars? Notice how almost nobody makes them. A few people design them and put in the minute level of subtle labor, but most of it is done automatically. Processing? A few workmen are needed to do the more intricate jobs, but everything else is done through automation. Even a cursory glance at the show How It's Made will reveal how almost every aspect of any job could feasibly be reduced to a mass machine lineup and a few human quality checks.

Why?

Why is it better to have a machine do most of everything instead of having a human do it? Why is it better to have machines pop up in fast food restaurants; automatic burger flippers and shake makers, instead of paying the workers a few dollars more?

Well, because humans suck, really. We take bathroom breaks, we get tired, we are not always reliable, we can show malicious compliance, we get sick, our muscles ache, we overlook things, we waste time, we are inefficient, and we have this lovely tendency to try to get the most product we can out of the least effort possible.

I'm sure most people reading this can recall a time when not everyone in a group project necessarily pulled all their weight, after all. Weight that a machine could pull effortlessly, and without excuses.

Please note, this is not to say machines are perfect. Wear and tear occur, they get malfunctions, mishaps, they're really quite expensive, and they can have trouble with seemingly stupid issues such as when a self-driving car is surrounded by salt and thinks the world is coming to an end. But note yet further: A machine doesn't have to be perfect. It just has to be better.

It just has to be better.

Humans are absolutely lovely things, the pinnacle of evolution. I don't doubt for a moment that if a machine and a human progressed equally as fast that they would never in a hundred thousand years catch up with us.

But we do not progress equally as fast.

There is archeological evidence to suggest that the average hunting party in your regular mud-hut village some odd stone-age number of years ago was fifty people. Because if you took along many more, you risked damaging group cohesion.

Today? The rough size of the average raiding party in WoW is fifty. The rough average battalion of soldiers is fifty. The rest of our physiological and psychological processes do not fall far from the tree.

. . .

Evolution is slow, grinding process; at more of a snail's pace than any layman could realize, and in this light, I worry about technology completely overtaking us in that way, in a way that is truly damaging.

Even now, the upper limit for how many people you can 'know', referred to as Dunbar's Number, is a rough one-hundred and fifty which, for a long time, was the size of the average gathering. For most of human history, villages numbered in less than a thousand people. You could theoretically be friends with everyone through *your* friends.

And now? We have seen more faces, spoken to more new people, people from all over the *world*, than our ancestors likely have in an entire lifetime. We associate ourselves with more people, we poll more people, you post something on social media and your single post is *seen* by more people than you could *ever* know.

When you think of that, that upper limit, the size of the tribe, the fact that your place in the tribe decided your likelihood of staying alive, and for that same breadth of time, your world was essentially the horizon. Whatever you saw, you claimed, and anything beyond it may as well not even matter.

That's why even today, a lot of our fictional stories about saving the world don't even FOCUS on 'The World', but a stark few people we're invested in, because THAT is what matters to our godless monkey brains.

We simply cannot fathom otherwise.

And so to have that, have those horizons open for us, to be greeted with the internet and have potentially tens of thousands of people screaming at us over any given thing. It is no wonder why some people get so depressed at being 'unpopular', their posts not going viral, their life not being as curated as those they see from all across the globe. It's no wonder so many people are so willing to do such stupid things for 'clout', for internet points, because our brains are convinced we are getting (or losing) the approval of a one-million strong tribe.

And it's no wonder why so many of us feel so lost and alone, suffering that isolation; because before, when you were a farmer or a candlemaker or a mason in your village, you saw the effects of your work, your efforts, building the town you lived in. Someone would buy your pottery and then you would SEE them carrying water in it. Someone would buy your food and then you would meet their children who ate it, often for generations to come.

Now?

So many people's work just deals with things so distant from them. Crunching numbers that they cannot possibly visualize as mattering for a corporation thousands of miles away.

Couple all this with the fact that the pace and improvement of technology grows at a half-life, always improving twice as fast in half the time, and the situation quickly begins to spiral. It grew much in the last thousand years, but it grew twice that amount in the last five hundred, so on, so forth until nowadays where you only need wait a couple of months for a major improvement to be made upon a machine that came out yesterday.

It took a bit over six thousand years from when civilization can be accurately described to be formed in order to build the airplane in 1903. The moon landing occurred a little over sixty years later. You should realize by now just how quickly humans can potentially be overtaken by automated machines that do the job, not perfectly, but still better than we do it.

"But that's a good thing, your lordship!" you might sputter, foolishly choosing to disagree with me. *"The more labour jobs machines do, the more people can focus on the BIG brain stuff or go into the arts!"*

Oh ho ho ho, dear strawman. Oh anime-girl-laugh indeed.

Human labour isn't just physical, it's also mental. Brain power, computation, imagination, all of these things go into intense calculations that allow for these machines to be built in the first place, that allow for architecture to be designed in the first place, that allow for people to decide on the very strains of food to grow in the first place. This is what is normally referred to as 'white collar' work. Big brain stuff.

Now that I described it that way; brain power, computation, and calculation; it is nothing short of foolish to even suggest that white collar jobs would be protected as mechanization advances onward. It is nothing short of foolish to suggest that robots couldn't possibly replace people in such thinky-thinky fields that every villainous robot in every sci-fi movie already ends up doing. People in such positions ALREADY rely heavily on computation to assist them in their practice, whether it's doctors, lawyers, bankers, brokers, politicians, teachers, or you, yes, just as you do.

This is more distinctive than technological progress, as progress has been happening for all of human history. One could argue that we have a historical precedent for why this spiritual defeat will not come to pass: cars were made and so horses became obsolete but we still *have* horses. Photography was invented but we still *have* landscape paintings. Lightbulbs are now cheaper than candles but candles *still* have their purpose. The film camera was made and yet we *still* have Broadway plays and musicals. Yes, this is all so, but A.I manufacture is different...

These things, these previous innovations in technology did not completely replace the old because they all assisted humans with a core task. Whether cart and buggy or horse or Chevy, all of these things still require a human driver.

What happens when they don't?

What happens when the 'human touch' is the tool being replaced?

"Ah! But creativity, Your Lordship! Creative fields shall remain untouched and humans can devote themselves to the arts!" some idealist will certainly

say, hands clasped, gazing toward the sun. Unfortunately, dear idealist, I have some bad news for you: The Arts are already being replaced.

Pindar Van Arman is a programmer, featured on Vice, who is already creating such tools for his robots; not just allowing them Artificial Creativity, but allowing any robot with the available software to do the same. CloudPainter is one such machine that is able to not only create original art but reportedly also remember what it has previously painted and improve upon it; and not just in artistic style either, but even noting which types of paintings, materials, and styles the market wants most of and replicating more and more of them.

An A.I almost won the 'Hoshi Shinichi Award' as part of a literary competition held in Japan. While it is worth noting that humans uploaded certain phrases and words for the A.I to use, as well as a plot-outline for how the novella would go, nigh the entire piece is the machine's own writing. And why not? Machines already excel in writing pieces with already firm frameworks. An artificial intelligence machine developed by graduate student Valentin Kassarnig of University of Massachusetts, Amherst, writes splendid political speeches; and Associated Press has partnered with the data-driven writing platform Automated Insights to begin automating quarterly earnings reports and select articles.

Machines have even written music. Of particular note is one named Shimon, who is able to study large data-sets of notes, as well as the works of previous musicians and then create its own completely original music; which it then plays. When originally created, Shimon was only intended to help 'improve' the music of musicians, helping them in their style, efficiency, to see what sells, etc., but through improvements to its design, it gained the ability to create its own music which, after being given a 'tick' or a groundwork of how the music should sound, is 100% its own and completely original (and also pretty good).

· · ·

It's easy to scoff and turn away to remark that each of these A. I's had human help and thus they will never 'truly' be creative, but at this point it's just wishful thinking. The human portion of these projects is minor, and as we already discussed, automated machines improve drastically every single year (and they improve with the help of automated machines as well). But even that is not the biggest threat; for if you have ever entered the arts, whether painting, drawing, writing, or composing, you would know just how difficult it can be to create a full piece and, despite all your effort and good intentions, it could still be sub-par. A limitation that A.I is not beholden to. It could have taken decades for you to become the next Van Gogh. It takes a machine a few minutes.

And It is worth noting that this essay was originally penned before the advent of either Art A.I like Midjourney or the chatbot ChatGPT; the former now being able to create fantastic works of art, and the latter being utilized to write full, college-level essays, both from as little as a simple prompt.

Wasn't technology first envisioned to try to help *us* do this? To give man space to do what is meaningful to them? And now, with the advent of even A.I voices, A.I writing, A.I chat bots, A.I music, A.I art, it seems as if we programmed these things to pursue *our* passions so *we* could do the boring busy work they were originally created to curb. Even the cover of this very book was made through a mixture of A.I art and photoshop. Not to knock it, of course, she's absolutely fantastic and adores the opportunities such new tools afford her, but the point is that it was done faster and cheaper than any human artist could have made from scratch... A fact that makes my other artist friends very nervous...

No wonder people feel so unfulfilled. They see none of the work they do in the world they live in all while the machines people swore would help them snatch their dreams out from under them instead.

. . .

Machines do not get distracted. They do not get uncomfortable. They do not need encouragement. They do not sit and tap pencils to their lips as they wonder what in the hell they're going to do. They just do it.

They can carve out in hours what would otherwise take weeks, months, or even years to create; and they suffer no burn out either. They're able to keep working, working, and working, with completely new and original pieces, forever.

The one final refuge of human safety is in the fact that these inventions are still relatively new; and all of them, from the brawn, to brain, to artistic ability of these robots, only exists in very niche environments with very specific opportunities to be truly practical; but this too is quickly changing. Machines get cheaper every single year, on top of already being more practical in these niche specialties; and these 'niche specialties' themselves are expanding as improvements are made. GPR's, or *"General Purpose Robots"* DO exist.

They are not pre-programmed beyond the basic essentials. Instead, they learn as they watch humans, and with the right attachments can do anything a human can with the only limitations being more finessed motor function; and even this is quickly changing. Think about just how vital computers are to the society we live in. All you need to do to change the specialty of a GPR is swap its software, and these will, inevitably, become as invaluable in the years to come as computers and cellphones are now.

For a point must be made here too that the general course of technology is ALWAYS onward; you can't just 'not' engage in it. Remember that cars were initially manufactured and sold as convenience machines to get where you wanted to go faster, but it was never necessary to buy one in order to live a relatively stable or active life; and now entire cities are built around cars and their logistics.

Already in many major cities of the world, it is widely regarded as not just impractical, but outright IMPOSSIBLE to get around without a motorized vehicle of some sort. It is the same with computers; where once computers were created and advertised as convenience machines, things you did not NEED but just made your job easier, it is now impossible for big businesses the world over to run without them.

You can already see sprinklings of this in social media as well; wherein social media such as Facebook was once started with the intention to connect with long-distance friends, it is now 'expected' that people have social media when they go to find jobs, for it is to be checked, and it is considered highly suspicious to not have one; actively locking you out of many professions depending on the temperament of the interviewer. It will come back around with the robot, which will not only be *better* than you, but also, much sooner than you think, *far cheaper*.

Still, there are some who suggest that this opening of the job market, you know, everyone getting fired and being replaced by robots, will just lead to better jobs for humans... but why? If a robot can already do everything you can do, better, with just a change in software, why would new positions opening due to innovation cause humans to be needed again? It wouldn't.

Even if anything new opened up, it would be a hop, jump, skip to next Tuesday where robots already filled the industry, again making humans useless once more. Historical patterns and recent growths (or lack-thereof) supports this, as where with every other technological boom was accompanied by an appropriate growth of new jobs and population, this is the first time in history where both new job creation and human population have not grown to match, and became stagnant.

Then again, maybe I'm wrong. Maybe humans are purists and would rebel against this coming age, trusting only human work to do most of anything. But big corporations don't care about that, now do they? Remember, something doesn't have to be perfect, it just has to be better.

Even if massive swaths of society rose up and boycotted massive mega-corps for its increasing reliance on A.I, it wouldn't matter even a tiny bit if the massive decrease in their costs for keeping those A.I outweighed the profits lost from your boycott. Besides, even if such a boycott WERE successful, you still have other nations who don't much care about pitiful little things like protests and would just go full automation anyways, far outclassing anything a non-automated nation could have in terms of output. Even if, say, one country alone went full automation, its growth in product and export, and the cheapness of it, would vastly outpace anything the rest of the world had to offer; forcing other nations to go full automation as well in order to remain economically viable or sinking into the dark; and we know this because it's exactly the same kind of rhetoric that surrounds the topic of 'Designer Babies'.

The thing that paves way for the future is convenience. Convenience will always win out over anything but the most die-hard fans of the old way, and I tell you, dear reader, that these robots will become far more convenient than you. It is only a matter of time.

"*So what,*" you might say, throwing up your arms. "*So robots begin doing everything, all humans are now useless, but the economy is better than ever. There is no want, no sickness, no famine, since robots do all the work and the prices are so low it would take mere pennies to buy enough of anything to feed three generations' worth of family as we all live in mansions. There would be no need for labor, people only working if they so choose, and then spending the rest of their time doing whatever they pleased! This is fantastic!*"
And you'd be absolutely right.
Aside from the glaring flaw of having the government give out a living wage to every person in a nation (that is to say, actually trusting the government to give you money 'just because' when many governments the world over would already force you into a mold if they could). It is very likely that a UBI (Universal Basic Income) would

be used as a ball and chain to keep people in line, with the threat of being denied your UBI as a deterrent to do anything a ruling party doesn't like.

But of course I'm being disingenuous. In ideal conditions, human corruption and incompetence aside, a full A.I takeover with all needs met sounds like a wonderful thing. Imagine! Never needing to work and having everything provided for you! Never having anything challenge you! Never needing to exert yourself for any reason! Just kind of... Sitting around... Waiting... For something... *Anything* to happen... In a world that's fully automated... Where everything is done for you... Hm.

See, I believe the world is going to end, but I'm one of those weirdos who thinks it will end, not due to a meteor strike or zombies or even because the robots rise up. I believe the world will reach an emotional Armageddon. I believe there will eventually come a time where people just ask themselves *"Why bother?"*

People already do, don't they? People already wait, sit, hope, pray for anything interesting to happen. They pray for Cthulhu to rise and for super-powers to suddenly crop up just so they have something interesting to do. They read and wish for adventure or play games to forget how bleak society seems. They talk about how they don't want to die, but instead wish that they had never been born. Brave New World. *Brave New World.* Where bravery is never needed, where nobody has to do anything, and that uselessness, that stagnation, drives people to murder just to see a more vibrant colour than the vast grey concrete we have all around us.

Imagine every aspiration you have becoming bunk, useless, pointless. Imagine your dream job, your dream hobbies, your dream life, but there is a machine that does each of them for you instead, more efficiently, and of a higher quality, and faster than you ever could. Why even bother?

The only way for humans to avoid this fate is to listen and reach a synthesis, becoming half machine ourselves and evolving just as quickly; but that just brings into question what the point is in trying to prevent our own obsolescence just to satisfy our own ego.

Why bother doing anything other than waiting for the end to arrive?

So, you see, dear readers, this is why I fear for the future, as much as I fear the future itself.

Because the Apocalypse is already here.

And it's happening right now… ish.

IS LIFE FAIR?

*T*he answer's no.
      Sort of.

This is gonna be an analogy in a minute, so stay with me for now.

Nobody but the most hopelessly deluded would ever conceive that life is fair. Bad things happen to good people. Good things happen to bad people. People are born into wonderful or terrible circumstances with no input from themselves or what they've done. Oftentimes it can feel as if success or failure, joy or sorrow, or even life and death can be decided all too frequently by factors completely independent of ourselves and our own decisions.

Life is not fair.

Yet at the same time, it almost feels premature to say it is *un*fair.

I was never fit to live, and mostly because I hate gambling. I hate chance and roulette wheels and the big roaring lights that try to deceive me into feeling like I accomplished something by pulling the level a little bit differently, maybe, and that's what caused me to win.

I also hate gambling because I am terribly unlucky. I seem to constantly be at the wrong place at the wrong time, not even in an interesting way, just a boring way where nothing cool happens. My paperwork is often misfiled or mislabelled the moment it goes back into the system, and my super important government papers stamped with big red [URGENT] letters have been delivered to the wrong address. Repeatedly. Businesses are closed for me despite saying they are open online, standards seem to be more strict upon my attempting them only to grow lax when I stop, and when I try to properly exercise I roll my ankle during a jog.

Even my D&D characters suffer. It is a running joke in my group that because I so constantly roll terrible attributes that I can just take them from the point system instead.

This is also why I never played Poker while I was in Basic Training. A very popular game. Often for money.

Though... describing Poker as a game of chance isn't entirely accurate either. Luck is a major factor. You have no control over the cards you are dealt. Whether good or bad, that's just the works. Realistically, they're entirely random. But you *can* control what you do with them. What you bluff. What you risk. How well you can profile others. That's why it's interesting to watch Poker Tournaments despite the actual deal itself being entirely out of the hands of the players. There is nothing but luck involved, but the skill comes in how that luck is handled.

And that's a lot like life, isn't it?

Luck, despite being... well, *luck*, is still, in a rather roundabout way... *fair*. SOMEONE had to be born the millionaire's kid. SOMEONE had to be genetically cursed. SOMEONE had to be naturally gifted. SOMEONE had to be born an addict. SOMEONE had to have the beautiful genes. SOMEONE had to have the weird fetish. It was just as likely to happen to you as it was to anyone else.

. . .

It seems then that the only conclusion *is* that life is fair. Perfectly fair. And that is the problem.

I once heard that one's politics in life depended heavily on the factor they believe luck played into each person's life. If they believed that someone could succeed despite poor odds with a bit of talent and willpower, they were more likely to favour traditionally 'independent' policies; while if they believed that the whole of your life could be determined by the mere flip of a coin, they'd be more utilitarian; and it is very easy to agree with both for entirely different reasons.

It seems wrong to try to instill the lesson that life is about luck. That they better hope they're lucky and that's about it. Some people are born winners into rich families like 'self-made billionaires' whose parents actually owned the company they worked at, while others are just born; lucky to scrape by enough to see what a good life *might* be like from afar. It seems wrong because we shouldn't be trying to instill that defeatism into people. We shouldn't be trying to convince them that their one chance came and went before they made their first decision. And we shouldn't convince them of that because it's also entirely *wrong*.

In the studies "*The Value of Believing in Free Will*", "*Prosocial Benefits of Feeling Free*", and "*You Didn't Have To Do That*", it was found that not only did those who had a deterministic view of life (as opposed to a belief in free-will) have worse quality-of-life traits than their counterparts; being more prone to adultery, poor mood control, and a sense of entitlement; but *also* that if you *undermined* someone's belief in their own free-will, they were at-risk to *develop* these same negative traits. Conversely, studies such as "*Subjective Correlates and Consequences of Belief in Free Will*", "*The Freedom to Excel*" and "*Personal Philosophy and Personnel Achievement*" all show a correlation between one's belief in their own autonomy, responsibility, free-will, and their overall quality of character. (Though it is worth noting that associations between one's free will and their position in life are complex; and in certain cases it is unknown which came first).

In light of this, it seems actively harmful to teach children that luck and circumstance is what shapes their life, and they shouldn't strive any bit beyond their station because life will slap them back down.

At the same time, however, it seems irresponsible to try to drill into people that if their life is horrid, all they need to do is work harder; as if too many avocado toasts and sleeping in an extra ten minutes is all that separated them from the local billionaire.

In fact, this kind of rhetoric is so-far removed from reality that in reviews from the Edelman Trust Barometer (a trust and credibility survey hosted by Edelman Data & Intelligence Firms, vey official looking), to polls on Twitter, and even to articles on Forbes, there is a common consensus that hard work no longer correlates to greater rewards, nor that it gives you a better life.

And with the Edelman Trust Barometer we can go even deeper. From 2022 to 2018 we can see that between all responders polled in developed markets worldwide, there was NO majority that believed their life would improve within the next five years. For the past half-decade, dissatisfaction with the media, government administrations, and corporations has only increased, and fewer and fewer people believed they would be helped by *anyone* if something bad happened to them, citing polarization as the main cause. This isn't an issue of Western kids being too 'pampered' and 'soft', it's a deep anxiety across the world. A world filled with nepotism, cut-throat economics, and where stocks going up means nothing for the common man while stocks going down means they lose their jobs.

It is irresponsible to teach children that they can avoid all of this if they just work harder, as if all the onus were on them.

"You get what you pay for," is a common saying, but it seems as if you don't always get what you work for. At least you still get something.

And maybe we should not view hard work as pulling ourselves up by the bootstraps alone, but even buddying ourselves up to the boss so that harsh nepotism can work for us instead. For life *is* a lot like a game of cards. There are some cards you want, some you don't, there are bad hands, there are good hands, and there are straight flushes that folded to a well-bluffed pair. A deck of cards isn't unfair because it gave one man a bad hand and another a good one. But maybe it's not fair either. Maybe that's just how it goes.

Life, such as it is.

In this, the only real difference is that you can't fold and reliably expect a new hand. Sometimes you're given a bad hand, and another, and another, and you just keep getting bled dry; and at such times it is certainly easy to think of folding entirely. Of leaving the table.

But there is a saving grace to life. And that is you cannot *lose*.

When you run out of poker chips, you are kicked from the table. When you draw your last card, you lose the game. When you mess up one too many hands you lose your money, your house, and perhaps even your family. But in a card game you're forced to quit. There is no such force in life.

Imagine playing that same poker game and betting absolutely everything on a hand and losing, you just ruined your life and may never get it back to the way it was. But you aren't kicked from the table. Instead, the dealer offers you a brand-new hand, and free chips to work with as you please, more time tomorrow, more opportunities to come; you'd be inclined to think it was the greatest poker table in existence, for what else would allow you to lose and yet always have a chance to regain what you lost and win even bigger.

There is a simple beauty in that. That no matter what happens, so long as you live, you can try.

So good luck or bad, fortune or misfortune, we are still here, still playing. So let us see within ourselves the power to try. So that maybe tomorrow might be better.

ON THE FOUR PILLARS OF LIFE WELL LIVED

*W*hen speaking of strength, any kind of strength, whether it revolves around a single person or an ideology or even the entire world, there is nothing more important to speak about than the four pillars.

These pillars are Truth (Both in the acquisition and pursuit of knowledge), Freedom (independence and the ability to make your own choices), Power (discipline, skill, superiority), and Justice (the ability to distribute restitution or retribution as seen fit).

Everything must exist in balance, which is why there must be four. To build up one is to build another, and to shatter one is to shatter another. You cannot build one to the neglect of the others, as more than just development is needed in each area, but comprehension. It is imperative to see the strings that bind them together, as each system itself behaves as a living thing. We all have needs, and we all wish to press on. You can imagine the universe being the body and the world just a cell, or the world being a body and a culture just a cell, so on, so forth, until we get down to you; right now, reading this, and we wonder how many worlds are within you right now.

. . .

The universe was created out of chaos. It was hectic and destructive, but even in the endless configuration of this infinite body, there was some order. As things become ordered they become familiar, expected, and there is something comforting about discomfort so long as you know what's uncomfortable; because there is order in chaos, but if order itself is to exist at all there must be something to compare it to. There must *be* chaos in order for things to *be* ordered. In order for there to be answers, things must be wrong. For things to be found, they must be lost. For strength to be gained, it must be weak. To shine a light is to cast a shadow; and so there is balance between these extremes.

Balance is necessary in everything, from the tiniest atom to the multiverse itself; it must be in balance for things to contest against one-another, to come into conflict and become strong. Things cannot grow if there is nothing holding them back. If there was no balance, only one dominating another, there would be only stagnation; order in a world that doesn't require it, or chaos in a world that doesn't notice it.

Dehydration and water-poisoning both result in death, but you must have thirst in order to drink and be healthy, and it is unhealthy to drink too much if you are already hydrated. Your muscles conflict against the force of your weight as your immune system conflicts against the outward bacteria and viruses, but if there were none, your system would be rendered useless and grow weak. The sun provides vital benefits to all living things whilst also killing them if they stay out in it too long. Things and even aspects must conflict and fight if they are to fulfill themselves; be it their purpose of existing such as a steel beam holding up a building or an emotional need such as a man who finds himself in nameless artwork.

. . .

You cannot find what is not lost, and you cannot realize the bigger picture until a part of it is removed and every little piece is affected. You must lose yourself before you decide to find yourself, you must be weak before you decide to be strong, you must be trapped before you can be free; the only difference between being free at first and being trapped and freeing yourself is the level of comprehension and understanding that comes with it. To starve and taste good food, and to nearly die and appreciate life; even if the food is rotten and life is unkind. There must be unbalance before you can balance yourself, and then the constant rate of growth versus the challenges you face mirror the balance you have in yourself while facing the unbalance of everything against you.

Order in chaos.
   Chaos in order.
   A universal flow that is achieved in every thing, every action, every push and pull; because it must be. An equal and opposite reaction from every action, for good or for ill.

You might ask yourself why people should be trapped at all, in lieu of being taught to appreciate being free, and it's the same reason you must touch a flame to understand the pain it brings regardless of how many times you are taught it would hurt you. Understanding must be achieved in order to grow in the ways you desire, but you cannot understand at all if there is no growth. This is what I mean when I say you cannot develop one pillar without the other; because they support eachother, just like every cell supports your body and every person supports a society; it expands larger and larger until the entire universe is covered and everything is acting as it should. Of course things go out of line and get a bit unbalanced, chaotic, but it's no different than having a virus in your body or a criminal in society; these things are necessary in order to develop; even the universe itself faces destruction against its person. Perhaps this is why it expands too.

To start, you must let go of the narrow view that 'extreme' only has context in politics or religion. Truly, an extremist is simply anyone with conviction toward an ideal. ANY extremist is dangerous, not because they disagree with you, but because they will do anything to see their ideal come to fruition. This is okay, there is nothing wrong with this act; for it is this very act that allows you to fight and grow.

You must understand that Good is not necessarily benevolent and might have no intention to help you, and likewise that Evil is not necessarily malevolent and might have no intention to harm you. The good in your world only seems so because of the views and ethics you share with them, and the evil is all that opposes you. An evil from a thousand years ago might seem mundane today. A good in a thousand years from now might seem horrific. A boulder is not evil for crushing you anymore than medicine is benevolent for curing you; and so it is the same with conflict. Morals change from person to person and what might be good to one is not so to another; because of this, while you can recognize evil and good in your life, you must not think of it as evil or good, but only as an action and reaction.

Do keep in mind that I am not referring to neutrality, where you hold no extremism, no strong views or convictions, take no strong action. I am referring to a type of 'universal balance', where instead of having no extremes, you simply pit one extreme against another. Understanding that for there to be a winner there must also be a loser. To gain, there must be loss. Though starvation and stuffing both result in death if taken too far, both are good ways to gain a desired outcome and the same can be said about ALL extremes and angles. The more you put into your ambitions, the farther they will take you, but the more you will lose in the process.

A man who wants to be the best can devote his life to absolute victory, and in doing so forsakes the average days, relaxation, and common luxuries. As a result, in order to avoid the emotional, spiritual, and sometimes physical death that comes with an extreme life, other extremes must be adopted. To train your body makes it strong, but to train it too much breaks down its healing and immune system; thus the strongest, fastest, toughest of people all know how to relax and slow down, even better than those who are lazy and never train at all. It is the smartest people who tend to enjoy the simplest of hobbies, the richest that can be the most frugal, the most well-travelled who's favourite place is home. They do this because in order to appreciate the fruits of your labour and accomplishments, you must be able to step back from it and turn your focus a little differently.

If a workman constantly builds upwards, when will he get the chance to stand back and look from the ground up? They must stop; step back, look, with a clear mind focused on a much larger picture rather than the next step. On a spiritual level, such actions are needed in order to reevaluate yourself; you must introspect, compartmentalize, wonder what type of person you are and want to be and if you are taking the steps required to get there. You must sacrifice everything you are to be everything you want to be. The problem is that many people do not know what they want. This is why conflict, extremism both outward and inward, must be faced, as you reflect your perspectives on everything you have experienced in life.

The meaning inscribed within the dark is not drawn from the abyss but drawn from the light that shines down in it. To understand, one requires contrast. How can you know you are brave whilst never experiencing fear? Going down this line, it is obvious that the more you experience and the more extremes you witness, the more defined and refined you become as a person, but *only* if you can perceive it correctly, the way the person you want to be would see it.

A person can go through a test a thousand times and fail each time because they never find out why they lose, while another person can go through only once and know exactly why they lost in order to correct it the next time. Experience means nothing; proper interpretation *of* your experiences is everything, and a proper interpretation is whatever gets you closer to your true goal. It doesn't matter if others do not approve of the course you take, this is just more conflict, more extremes for you to overcome, and you do so by taking on another extreme: The 'yes' to the 'no', the 'permit' to the 'deny'.

Look around you at those in your life or those you knew, think of how many people did not follow this law, think of how many people never felt the need to improve themselves or their standing. Look at the people who hold no convictions, who have no extremism in them, who have never made an enemy in their life over their beliefs. Do they truly seem developed? Do they truly seem whole?

The difference between neutrality and balance is that while the former *negates* equals and opposites, the latter *encourages* them. But this too is a type of balance. I do not expect you to reach enlightenment or shake hands with a god. You do not have to master a total Zen look on life in order to complete this philosophy. All you must do is devote yourself to what you want to be and understand that opposition and conflict must be faced in order to achieve this.

For every fanatic there is a skeptic, for every friendship there is a hostility, for every life there is death, for every winner there is a loser; this philosophy is not about being all of these, it's about understanding that there WILL be all of these, that all of these are okay and merely ambivalent rather than positive or negative, and that by facing them, you develop into something beyond them; but to do that you must devote yourself to that one thought, that one image, you yourself, the way you want to be: The perfect version of you.

And we start by finding the truth.

We will focus on the pillar of Truth first: What it is, and why it is necessary. Most people only see truth in a 'material' sort of way, like a tangible weapon they can pick up and face toward their foe; but in reality, truth lies with everything and in all things. It is indestructible, absolute; once something is made true it cannot be false again. Even if the truth is forgotten it doesn't make it any less real or complete, and so while truth may be covered up or twisted to suit propaganda or perception, it can never truly be broken.

This is what makes truth so important and why it is so valuable. Why so many people want the bedrock of truth on their side. Why so many use it as a type of power-word, as if it were an incantation; because to have such a rigid ally is a powerful thing indeed. In order to discover the truth of the world surrounding you, you must first bring out the truth in yourself; focusing on what type of person you are and who you want to be, your abilities and your limitations both, and how you can become this idealized version of yourself.

This is achieved through deep introspection, meditation, and insight, and while you may uncover some very uncomfortable things about yourself, this is absolutely required in order to grow and develop as a person. You must ask the questions about yourself that you are afraid to answer. You must face the insecurities you never wanted to admit to. You cannot fix yourself if you cannot admit fault. You cannot find right if you refuse to see wrong. As it is above so it is below.

After you discover the truth within yourself you will find life comes much easier to you. Without the subconscious blocks you place upon yourself in order to avoid discomfort or emotional pain, you will be able to embrace all things, good and bad, and realize why you do as you do and believe as you believe; and when THAT is achieved, you may find the will to change it. If you *wish* to change it.

"Man cannot remake himself without suffering, for he is both the marble and the sculptor."
   – Alexis Carrel.

After this you will be able to find the truth in other things rather than the false propaganda others might feed you. By virtue of your own internal light, your willingness to see through your own lies, it becomes that much easier to see through the facades of others in turn. You see this by seeing past what they say and instead seeing the motivations of why they say it. The doubts they may harbor. The fears they may hide.

By knowing yourself, applying what you learned in your soul searching to outside investigation, and being able to search your subconscious for answers, you will be able to bypass most bias toward information; you will be able to know probability and likelihood and answers to all that you ask will come easier as well.

If all goes well for you, you might even be able to share this newfound wisdom with others; but beware, not everyone is so inclined to the truth and some might refuse to see it while others will fight you to protect the lies they tell themselves. You must be cautious before using up your limited energy trying to convince someone, for they may not want to be convinced regardless.

Recognize that nobody will ever believe something they do not want to believe no matter how much evidence is put in front of them and only ever seek truth, both objective and subjective, in order to grow and change yourself, not others. If others are kindred spirits they will follow you, and if not, you needn't concern yourself with them. Truth will reach all corners eventually, it's only a matter of time; and it is not always your duty to try to show them the way. You may still be *wrong*, after-all. And there is still something to be learned from misinformation.

. . .

In "The Knight in Rusty Armor" by Robert Fisher, there is a section where the titular Rusty Knight is trapped within a maze of darkness from which he cannot escape. Between his bouts of terror and grief, he comes to terms with his own cowardice and lack of resolve, and in doing so, finds a small glow upon the floor. Using it, he is able to make his way a little better through the maze and eventually find his way out.

In speaking with the Merlin of Arthurian legend, it is revealed that the maze was, in fact, a representation of his own psyche. That the darkness was his lack of self-knowledge, that which he did not know even about himself. Are you able to know anything you want about yourself? Why you have the nostalgia you do? Why you have the fears you do? Why you dream what you dream? Are you able to face all answers about yourself no matter how boastful or uncomfortable they make you? Are you able to face your own darkest secrets and brightest ambitions? Absolute clarity is not necessary. There is always more to learn and discover and new ways to grow. It is the *attempt* that is necessary, and as you develop as a person you will gain new truths to uncover and explore. It does not make you unwise to not have all the answers. Nobody does. The wisdom comes from the pursuit of them.

One must always remember that if you have to bend the truth in order to get the answers you desire, not only will your answers still be false; but you will be putting effort into a falsehood that will ultimately lead nowhere. Truth will be hard to accept sometimes, but we are only deceiving ourselves if we allow ideology or bias to blind us to what the world shows is true, and if your goal is so hard to reach that you feel you must either bend the truth or ignore it outright when it doesn't agree with you, then perhaps it is the goal and not the truth that should change.

. . .

All hurt gained from truth and fact can easily be avoided, both inside us and in the world around us, as long as we remember to develop beliefs based on the knowledge we have already acquired rather than develop the beliefs first and then seek out the knowledge to prove it. You develop the theory after the fact, not before.

With this insight gained, clarity is found; and through clarity comes freedom.

The Pillar of Freedom comes second, though it is no less important than the first. When the blinds are removed and you can see the world clearly, you can see exactly what binds you down and move to escape from it. Some might question why freedom is necessary for personal and societal growth, and the answer to that can be found in nature itself. Any creature that has ever existed can never grow larger than the container that it's in without risk of serious harm; so too does it follow for ideas, art, and emotion. If you lock these things away and keep them down where they are unable to develop past a certain point, they simply won't.

Physical freedom, to act as you please. Financial freedom, to use what you earn. Mental freedom, to dream and question without fear. Spiritual freedom, to believe and practice your ideals and intuitions as you see fit. All these things are required in order for someone to be truly independent. But take care! Freedom to do as you please does not mean freedom from consequences; indeed, consequences and responsibility are a PART of freedom, not restricting to it. The more responsibility you have and the greater consequences you might face, the more control is in your hands, and note that you do not necessarily have to care about the consequences.

A being so large that it can crush entire colonies of insects without a second thought has many consequences to their actions, but they're also so large that they might not even consider or suffer from them. On the other hand, to avoid responsibility and consequences both belittles and demeans you, makes you incapable of making choices or comprehending them.

Look at those who dodge their responsibilities, who shirk their duties and find any excuse as to avoid blame or punishment for their conduct. Do they seem emotionally stable? Happy? Mature? Would you trust them to work beside you, or under you? Would you depend upon them for matters of importance or substance? Do you look upon these people and idolize them and want to be like them? Then you must see why you should do away with the desire to avoid work, responsibility, and consequence. As all these things are absolute necessities in order to gain freedom.

To be free of these things means dependence; it means that someone else takes care of you, decides what kind of work you do, limits you in terms of choice or finance. One might try to convince themselves that if they are free from responsibility, they can do as I like; but it is not so. NOBODY is free from responsibility. From the moment you are born, or something is created, someone, somewhere, is convinced you owe them a favour. Whether this is actually true or just their entitlement doesn't matter, for to be hounded by debts, real or imagined, is only barely short of having the debt itself.

If you must run from those who might injure you or cause you inconvenience, it is not a sly man escaping his chains but a slave trying to run from the master. Note: While it may limit you if someone thinks you owe them, by no means are you obligated to serve them if you know you should be free. In the event you find yourself in these situations, do not fret or run for cover but stand boldly and firmly at your post. A person who owes nothing should think carefully before they run instead of facing it. And whatever you do, above all else, you must not give in to this forced imposition of servitude, that you really *do* owe them, because whether they are a creditor coming to collect debt on behalf of another or a pushy family member who demands conformity, if you try to placate them by giving them *some* of what they want, it will only embolden their entitlement to *all* of it.

It may seem counterintuitive to say that taking on duties and responsibility *adds* to your freedom rather than detracting from it, but in taking on responsibility, you are not placing yourself in the service of another but giving *yourself* more leverage. If you take on the responsibility of doing a task, then you are the arbiter of how that task gets done; and any attempt to impede you could be met with a forceful rebuke, that they are free to find another; or you may give them a hand-waving dismissal, assuring them that you shall change even while you continue on your course.

Most people are not concerned with the logistics of a project, they only become anxious about being caught in the blast if you fail. If you either prove that they won't be, or refuse to allow failure, you would be surprised at just how much control you can wrest unto your powerbase.

Think to yourself on the many righteous leaders throughout history who held the most power and control and yet always considered themselves servants of their people; and it would be foolish to suggest this mindset diminished their freedom. Even many of the people you yourself may know who consider themselves free as a bird and without a care are actually tied to many things which would prevent their escape or growth, even if they wanted it.

But be warned. There is a very big difference between serving a group or ideology and being dependent upon it. Submitting yourself can be viewed as an act of duty and honour, and justified upon the grounds that it allows for opportunities and growth in the areas you desire them; but dependence denies both growth and opportunity; since those who depend on *you* will use their leverage over you to keep you in that position.

You can be dependent upon something in all the ways you can be free. Physical dependence can be in the form of addiction, financial dependence can be in the form of loans, emotional dependence can be in the form of another person or idea, and so the list goes on. In order to avoid these traps you must be mindful about your willpower and self-discipline; understand that there are many things in this life DESIGNED to have you dependent upon them and be mindful of where your wants, needs, and self-image comes from.

To help check yourself or others for these types of dependency, think of yourself in three dimensions: Past, Present, and Future. If your present self is taking from your future self (that is to say: Time/Money/Pleasure your future self could have had) with the expectation that it must be paid back, then it is a dependency trap. If something offers you instant gratification now, and favours to pay it back in the future, it is a dependency trap. If there is anything that gives now, and takes later, it is a dependency trap. Avoid these in ways that diminish you. Accept them in ways that strengthen you.

I reiterate that freedom is not always reflected in the physical world. You must also be free of personal insecurities and delusions, free of thoughts and bad feelings that plague your consciousness, free from spiritual suppression and unlawful condemnation; but, by the power of truth, you will already have the means to free yourself from all these things and more. Break free of these chains, and when you do, you can become powerful.

The Pillar of Power comes third, gained through being able to express your will and stretch your influence across horizons both internal and external. However, like the first two, Power is often misunderstood by those who seek it, and thus they never quite find it. Power is not something that can be bought (though sway can be), power is not something that can be goaded out of people (though wealth can be), and power is not something that is gained through the servitude of others (though luxury can be).

You might look around you and disagree, seeing bribery and extortion and bias all around you, you might very well think that power is *clearly* something that can be gained easily or with enough friends. But hark. You cannot bribe a tongue not to stutter. You cannot threaten a flood to recede. You cannot hold influence over a two-hundred-pound weight. Two hundred pounds will always be two-hundred pounds, regardless of who picks it up or why, and THAT is power; standing firm and rigid against all things.

Being able to tell your body 'no' when it wants to give up or being able to earn the loyalty of others, not through gold but through shared idealism, mutual respect, and admiration. You cannot build strength without dedication and discipline, and nobody but you can earn that strength for you; so it is the same with intelligence, or willpower, or charisma, or knowledge, or true friends.

Nobody but you can hold these things and nobody but you can earn them, to try to gain them any other way than by your own effort will always result in failure. Indeed, no matter how capable or firm someone might seem, always be aware of outside powers keeping them afloat, and thus which powers they remain beholden to. If someone has not earned their powers and cannot keep them of their own accord, their strength is not true strength, but something that's dependent upon the whims of circumstance; and can be lost just as quickly.

Anyone can imagine themselves ferocious with the right equipment. Anyone can imagine themselves clever with the right connections. Anyone can imagine themselves brave when they are protected from consequences. But what are you without these things? What are you when you only have your own strength to depend upon?

. . .

You will do well to remember that while discipline can be in the form of body, mind, spirit, and surroundings; power must be exercised over ourselves first and foremost. Nobody can respect someone who does not first respect themselves, and nobody can be led by someone who is unable to lead themselves. To be able to conquer nature, people, and aspects, you must first be able to conquer your OWN nature, your own character, and your own aspects; to be able to absolutely define and redefine what you are as needed and adapt to the experiences in your life.

Know that you are a reflection of your perceptions and values. Are you proud of who you are? Are you proud of how you have handled the challenges in your life? Look around you and see what troubles you and what makes you happy; are these things truly worth your time and effort? If everything wrong with your life was fixed right now, would you be happy or just find other pains? If everything right in your life was ruined, would you be miserable or find other joys?

There is an old fable I enjoy, of the Warlord and the Monk. So the story goes, a warlord of times long past was to receive tribute from a local village; and when he did not receive it, he flew into a rage uncontrollable. He set his forces upon this town, salting the earth, destroying the very crops and lands he could have made use if with just a little more foresight, before marching to the top of their highest hill and into their monastery where the local Monk sat, meditating.

The Warlord approached the Monk, who did not stir even as the heavy greaves echoed upon the soft wooden floor, who did not stir even as the Warlord raised the tip of his blade and placed it over the Monk's heart.

And seeing the Monk unmoved, the Warlord scoffed. *"Don't you realize I can run you through without blinking an eye?"*

Whereupon the Monk finally responded. *"Don't you realize I can be run through without blinking an eye?"*

And so the two wait, frozen in time, even still.

When it was told to me, it was told in the tone of the superiority of the Monk, though I do not believe this is so. Patient though he was, willpower though he had, his village still burned, and he could do nothing to stop it. But neither is the Warlord superior, who sowed the seeds of his own starvation in the very fury that he could not control.

In this, the Monk represented to me a sense of power over oneself. While the Warlord represented power over the world. If you have power over others, yet not of yourself, you are no better than a child throwing a tantrum, or a raging beast whose strength and fury is unfocused, impotent. Likewise, if you have power over yourself, yet not over others, you will always be beholden to those who could blow you back and forth with the might of the wind or trample your efforts underfoot with the rake of their hooves.

Instead, one must be *both* the Monk and the Warlord. One must have power, and then have the self-control and wisdom to use that power effectively, in accordance with their will over the world.

Many of the highest kings were brought low because they could not control their own impulses. And many of the most enlightened of men were kept to heel because they constantly had to appeal to others to gain influence.

Discipline of mind is attained through discipline of the mind. It sounds redundant, but it's the easiest way to think about it. Delayed gratification. Self-restraint. Going out of your comfort zone. Controlling how you react to the emotions you feel. Even something as simple as sitting and breathing, without distractions, discarding your brain's cravings for stimuli, can be an act that enforces your will. And it will serve you well.

After that comes discipline of body. Can you run if you need to? Can you fight? Can you muster the motor control to master the instruments you look so wistfully upon? Can you endure pain if you are called to do so? The more abilities lay within your arsenal, whether it be fundamentals like swimming or riding a bike, or more advanced skillsets like operating heavy machinery or using another language, all of them open doors for you that were shut before; because to have the *ability* to do something is to have more *options* in how to ensure a thing is done.

After this still comes discipline over the world around you. The plants you allow to grow in your garden. The animals you are capable of handling. The rhetoric you employ to spread your ideals and the subtle strings you pull to ensure people act and react as you desire. This is why personal strength is so important, since it will also act in accord with the connections you form with the world. People naturally gravitate toward strong people. The strong relate to the strong, the weak admire the strong, and the low worship the strong.

It is your choice to decide what you want to do with these people, whether to share your insight and discipline with them or to rule them and be satisfied that you are fulfilling their whims of having all responsibilities stripped from them.

People who want power will always be your friends as people who envy it will always be your acolytes. Even those who fear power, who will be your enemies, are nothing to concern yourself over; for the greatest of strength will allow even the greatest of failures to slough off you like melting snow. You can rebuild and try again.

It is worth noting that in this regard, even the maladies you suffer will not hold you back. There are defects, mental and physical, that will act as a barrier to one path or another; and yet much like how the blind have their other senses heightened, so too shall your horizons stretch outward as you find methods to make up for your limitations. So long as you can see the path you want to walk, you have within yourself the power to do so.

Power and discipline are required for any and all development; as nothing can last without power. People can choose not to listen to truth, and people can choose to deny freedom, but *nobody* can deny force. When you ask, it is to the discretion of the asked to provide. When you demand, and have the force to back it up, there is no discretion needed. This is why it's such a useful and necessary thing. Like a messenger who delivers even to the most well-hidden and reluctant of people, power is something that cannot be ignored; as the more of it there is, the more those around it will listen.

Note that power is necessary even if you are pacifistic in your methods, as power is required for absolute defense too. Even if you are the most noble of people, there are those out there who would gladly use any type of trickery or edge to bind you; and thus having power will even the odds. Power gives you the ability to not only talk, but be heard. Any type of conflict or challenge you have will be easier the more powerful you are and any type of person who wants your favour will think twice before trying to force it. Are you already so capable? If someone threatened you, or bribed you, or taunted you, could you resist and hold firm? If someone had more power and the willingness to use it, could you walk away unscathed? Your loved ones? Your livelihood? Is the full extent of your abilities sufficient for the life you want to live?

It's incredibly easy to gain social power and influence; the problem is with keeping it. Look around you and see how many shirk their duties, their responsibilities, who are so willing to cast off their authority onto the back of another; and think of how much you could gain by taking them up. Think of how grateful those around you would be when you did so. That is why keeping power is difficult, because once you have it, it is easy to rest on your laurels. It is even easier to cower at the bright light and tall heights and wish to be closer to the Earth.

That is why people give it away for the chance to rest. And yet at the same time it is even harder to be weak, to feel so empty and disappointed, to have to constantly find lesser and lesser ways of exacting your will. People convincing themselves that true happiness is one more minute in bed, one more minute relaxing, one more minute with luxury, but you can have these things at any time. They are not measures of material wealth, but a lack of mental pressure. To acquire power in order to gain them is putting the cart before the horse.

These petty delights, these hits of instant gratification, must be done away with, for it is worth it even though it may not seem like it in the moment. The benefits such effort will yield down the road of life far outweigh any inconvenience it places you in now. Even if you spend your entire life pursing this path and have nothing to show for it, you are still better off than a living man who died twenty years ago when they decided to settle. Truly, is there even such thing as a failure who honestly tries? Is there such a thing as effort or toil that would ever betray you?

It seems difficult, but there are always opportunities. Is money your concern? Observe how the wealth maneuver their finances to better grow their capital and follow their example. Invest. Be decisive and ask for raises. Ask for promotions and greater responsibilities. Make your desires known. The squeaky wheel gets the grease. Is your sense of worth what makes you timid? Then you must temper yourself into something you would admire.

Exercise. Do not give in to temptations. Do what you've been putting off. Do what you say you will do. Is the fear of failure holding you down? There is no such thing as perfection. There is no such thing as a perfect track-record. There are no such things as no losses and no setbacks. To encounter external obstacles does not reflect poorly on your internal resolution. Listen to people, the meek and powerful, see how they talk, the words they use, the places they congregate, the way they hold themselves and notice there is a pattern in all of it, and know that their actions are not a symptom of success but the cause of it. Follow their example, and once you have become powerful, you can seek out justice.

Justice taken by the hands of the people is, and has always been, the personification of forceful karma. Universal balance. Because our ideals of justice differ from person to person, and only the stronger gets their way, in the end the only TRUE justice is balance; one good for one evil, one right for one wrong, one reaction to one action. As justice does not have to be benevolent or malevolent, it can be handled by both types of people; taking the eye of a good man or the tooth of an evil man is still, at the end of the day, an eye and a tooth in your pocket; and their vengeance will rise up and return the favour upon you, or others, or the world itself.

What is morality? What is good and evil? Where does it come from and who does it favour? Is it better to be righteous, or good? Is an evil man who keeps their word nobler than a good man who lies to meet their ends? Is a woman of diligence more capable than a woman of compassion

Picture the heart of evil, something with absolutely no redemption or hope in its future, something completely devoid of all benevolence and humanity; now make it honest and diligent, imagine it to be loyal and polite, imagine it with gentleness, without any desire to intimidate or belittle those around it, that it is patient and humble, make it thoughtful and open, incorruptible in design and unfailing in feature, with all of its mannerisms and insights geared toward purity in its character. Would it even be an 'evil' thing at all? What would it say to you? What would it want? What would it think of you? Would it even care at all? If you imagined the heart of goodness with the exact opposite traits, would the answers be the same?

One must realize that in regard to morality and the ideas of good and evil, malevolence and benevolence are strictly independent of both. Evil does not have to hurt, and good does not have to help. Likewise, one can be evil while still being a righteous and devout person, as purity of heart and intention has no bounds on morality, but only ethics and virtue; neither of which is dependent upon the goods or evils of the person.

This is, of course, not permission to go and do evil acts and justify yourself with righteousness that doesn't exist, or to do good acts and then act like an honest person despite frequent deception; it is only a reorganization and comprehension that there is more to being good and evil than kindness and cruelty, and we have reason to be mindful of both. If too much good is done, people may become complacent and weakness is spread, but if too much evil is done, people may become hopeless and unethical in their conduct.

One must be able to face all goods and evils without seeing it as a personal attack or duty, and also understand that 'good and evil' are not tangible objects, but ideas to serve as a background for how we perceive ourselves and the world around us. This is a moral balance, to be able to comprehend both, appreciate both, adhere to one or the other, and still understand that these things are points of view relative to the world we live in.

Much like how truth requires that you are unbias, and freedom requires that you have been chained, and power requires self-discipline, justice requires that you do not see things in terms of 'good and bad', but only right and wrong and *why* you see them that way. Is it right to help others even if it means taking their own challenges away from them? Is it wrong to commit brutality in order to make a point and deter others from trying to commit greater acts of harm? Is it right to take revenge against those who have transgressed against you, even for the slightest offences? If not, what is justice at all? When is justice justified?

To take revenge and to pay dues is only keeping the balance that the universe itself desires to sustain. Just as you cannot have order without chaos, you cannot have good without evil; there must always be a reflection and conflict, otherwise it all becomes meaningless. For revenge to be proper, something wrong must have been done, and for dues to be paid, something right must have been witnessed; as such it is only right to act in a way that returns the action, to take one more chip out of the marble block of character until the masterpiece of clarity and purity finally shines through.

As such, do not feel distraught when you are called upon to destroy, nor feel over-burdened when you are asked to create; so long as your revenge is justified and your blessings help others to learn and grow, it will build to something greater.

Hold yourself to your highest standard of virtue, never bending or yielding to the ebb of influence, never seeking to do unnecessary help or harm, and always reacting so that hero or villain can live, learn, and thrive after the lessons provided. Do this, and you will always walk on the path of justice.

And with balance achieved, all parties held equal, it is all the easier to ferret out the truth.

As a final thought… At this point the process simply repeats itself, as there is always more to learn and always more to discover. It flows into a cycle that never ends, but always lets you grow. It is you and only you who decides, in the end, how far and wide you want to grow and what influence you want to reach.

You do not have to reach the end of this cycle to find fulfillment, only to practice it; for when you follow the path of truth, what lies hold sway over you? When you have ever-expanding knowledge at your back, there is no amount of deceit or manipulation that will keep it forever from your sight.

When you follow the path of freedom, what chains ever bind you? The very fact that they seek to lock you away screams to the point that you are free and will always be free, for there is no restraint over the mind and spirit.

When you follow the path of power, what weakness ever holds you down? Knowing that every challenge you face, every experience you undergo, every thought you form to your character serves you, and only you; to recognize that you have the potential to be the person you were always meant to be.

When you follow the path of justice, what forces can ever throw you off course? Knowing that you fight with integrity and the morality of all things, what claims to your goodness or evil will ever have effect? Knowing that everything you do is done to set things right.

No longer will you ever be restrained. No longer will you ever doubt your path. Neither word nor blade nor bullet can ever cause you destruction, as when you follow the path of the universe, there is no physical death that can ever hold you back. No tarnishing of your name or manipulation of the public that can do you harm. For you are one with all things and all things shall find their way to the universe just as you have, and they will see that you were right, just as we hold to the words and the dreams and the integrity of the beloved dead who fell so long ago, even to this day, and forever onward.

TO BE HAPPY

To be happy, to be truly happy, no matter what despairs befall you, you need only do two things: Focus on gratitude, and appreciate what you have.

That's it.

The problem is that people see happiness as something gained, something that needs to be attained objectively; they say,

"Oh, if only I had _____ or _____ I would finally be happy!"

but it doesn't work like that and it never will, for when we long for what we lost or yearn for what we crave more than we appreciate what we have, despair becomes inevitable.

You can be content with a position, or satisfied with something the same way that eating a large meal satisfies an appetite but being satisfied with fullness is not the same as enjoying the meal, nor is satisfaction the same thing as happiness. It is just as I said before: If you are not happy *without* something, you will not be happy *with* something, and it is because happiness is not something grasped from the ether, but something felt. It is something inside of you, burning like a fire that you need to fuel for yourself. It comes from appreciating what you have even if all you have is your life.

This is why you see people who seem to have everything and despite all their wealth and status they are absolutely miserable; and likewise you see people who seem to have the worst fortunes and yet they never find a chance not to smile. Because happiness is something that cannot be attained with money, or status, or power, or discipline, or affection, or anything of the sort no matter how much comfort these things give. Because even comfort is not happiness.

You are the common denominator of everything in your life and only you can make yourself happy. No outside object can, no other person can, and no achievement or reward can. Only you and it has only ever been you. It is easier to cry in a nice car than a poor one; and it is easier to find happiness when you do not have to worry about bills and basic needs, this is true; but the fact remains that there is no circumstance of life that cannot be improved upon with the mindset of gratitude and appreciation.

Even when you're trying to achieve a dream, you can at least convince yourself that the dream is what will make everything come together. But after you have it, you have no explanation or reason as to why you're still sad. The only thing that can truly make you happy is you, and you can only do that by having gratitude at even the simplest of things. You can only be truly fulfilled when chasing your dream is as satisfying as reaching it. Nothing else would do.

People always try looking for a deeper or hidden meaning behind things, but sometimes the answer is so simple that we smack ourselves for not figuring it out sooner. It doesn't take a god, or a hero, or a saviour to tell you the truth; all it takes is a bit of sense. The wisdom you yourself could achieve.

This is also the road to fulfillment; as happiness is something achieved inwardly, fulfillment is achieved by clutching at your passions and dreams, and those passions and dreams are cultivated through soul-seeking, discovering your destiny, and even the meaning of life. To begin, you need only to know where your principles are set, to find something you can live to achieve. Though that may just lead back into the search for the meaning of life.

So let me save you some time.

The meaning of life is to exist. That's why we're here. We came in upon a whim or on the backlash of an accident and so we grew out from nothing and will continue to do so as we are meant to. Our meaning is self-affirming. Our purpose self-evident.

But that's not really the question, is it?

The question people mean to ask is:

"What is the meaning of MY life?"

Well lucky you, I still have an answer for you.

The meaning of your life is whatever gives your life meaning.

And as for what gives your life meaning? I'm not sure. That's something that you will have to figure out for yourself.

ALSO BY JONATHAN CUE

The Journeys of Mal Malin Book 1: Apprentice

In all the Borean Colonies, fifteen-year-old Mal Malin is the last person you'd ever suspect as a wizard's apprentice. His ice freezes the spit in his own mouth, his divination won't work past the wall, and the last time he tried communing with an automaton, it chased him down the street.

But there is one thing the young noble does better than anyone else. Mal can raise the dead. A pity, then, that bragging about his Necromancy would only net him a one-way trip to the gallows.

Mal has already been plucked from the gutter and thrust into a world in which he does not fit. Can he guard his secrets? Or will he be ground beneath the weight of a world that hates him?

Apprentice may be Jonathan Cue's debut young adult dark-fantasy novel and the first book in "The Journeys of Mal Malin" series, but this slow-burn, contemplative and captivating tale about goodness, cruelty, loss and redemption is sure to leave readers spellbound.

ABOUT THE AUTHOR

Jonathan Cue is a royal dream spirit existing somewhere between the North Pole and the star Polaris.

This can be a rather long way to pass through, and so the most effective way to catch His Majesty's attention, whether to assist in world dominion or to make business inquiries, is to show a token of good will by performing good deeds around your community and then sending an email to:

jonathancue123@gmail.com

Printed in Great Britain
by Amazon

While attending a lecture given by Wil-Sannu of Babylon, Jonathan Cue received an assignment: seek out and report on how to correct the problems observed in the great city.

He found the problems were many, and since they were caused by a lack of wisdom, no solution would keep them from arising again. When the Achaemenid Empire fell, he watched history repeat itself as the same problems came back to haunt the next generation of kings and commoners both. Could it not be that if people were wiser, so many of these problems could be resolved altogether?

It is through this epiphany that Cue decided a lack of wisdom periled all things, and thus this collection of lessons and insights alike was assembled, in the hope that through the cultivation of wisdom, we may not only solve the problems of the past, but might yet avoid the problems of the future...

ISBN 9798393904524

9000

9 798393 904524